But I Should Be Fine

How to gain relief from anxiety,
overthinking and pesky self-doubt

Zoe Clements

Grounded Publishing

First published 2021 in the United Kingdom by
Grounded Publishing

ISBN 978-1-8382920-0-3 (print)
ISBN 978-1-8382920-1-0 (ebook)

DISCLAIMER

The purpose of this book is to educate, entertain and
provide information on the subject matter covered. All
attempts have been made to verify the information at the
time of publication, and the author does not assume any
responsibility for errors, omissions or other interpretations
of the subject matter. The purchaser or reader of this
book assumes responsibility for the use of this material
and information. The author assumes no responsibility or
liability on behalf of any purchaser or reader of this book.
The book contains no client case material and all examples
have been created to illustrate a point of learning. Any
teaching and learnings that are shared within the book have
benefited a number of clients and do not in any way identify
those clients.

Contents

Dedications

To all the brilliantly beautiful clients whom I have learned so much from over the years. You have inspired me more than you can ever know. Thank you from the bottom of my heart.

To the lovely Jane Travis, who knew I could write a book even before I did, and to Dale Darley, who steered me through my writing journey; this book wouldn't exist without you. I'm grateful beyond words.

Last but never least, this book is also dedicated to my gorgeous wife Lucinda, and my very cute but sometimes troublesome dog, Paddy. I couldn't have even attempted this chapter in my life without your unconditional love and support. Thank you for being you.

Introduction

But I should be fine.

EVERYBODY

At the age of 10, I experienced my first, and only, panic attack. I was mid chess match (yep, you heard that right) when I suddenly felt like I couldn't breathe. Much to my opponent's dismay, I abandoned the game and made a beeline to the nearest bathroom, where I promptly slid down the wall gasping for breath. It may have happened over 30 years ago, but I can vividly remember the terror I felt in that moment. As I put my hands to my throat, gulping in more air, my Mum came flying through the door and hugged me, and then the memory fades.

From the outside looking in, my 10-year-old self should have been fine. I had a roof over my head, food on the table each night, two parents and I was living the middle-class dream, residing in a town with access to a great education and, erm, a chess club. I was privileged. There was no horrific incident in my past, no big trauma to speak of. However, this panic attack was a sign I was far from fine, and it was just the beginning.

By the time I catapulted into my twenties, the signs were coming thick and fast. First off, my brain had gone rogue; I had always had a tendency to overthink, but now it was also noisy and critical. I had nagging self-doubt, which hung around like a bad smell, always concluding I wasn't good enough, regardless of the facts. To make matters worse, I was constantly anxious and full to the brim with uncomfortable feelings, which stuck around no matter how much I tried to numb them with chocolate and wine. To top things off, I didn't help myself. I was a walking, talking, people-pleasing machine, laser-focused on giving others what they needed, to the point of being neglectful of my own mental, emotional and physical needs. Again, from the outside looking in, I should have been fine. I was earning a decent wage, working in a swanky office in Canary Wharf and living the high life in London. However, the truth was I was far from fine.

In my late twenties, through luck rather than judgement, I stumbled onto a path that ultimately changed my life. I fell into volunteering on a helpline, leading to a career in counselling. I say luck rather than judgement because I never thought I would see a counsellor, let alone become one; after all, I thought, I should be fine. Fortunately, I found my way to the client's chair, and my time there, as well as my counselling training, was instrumental in helping me understand why I was suffering, despite all seeming to be well. Gaining this awareness was a tremendous relief; for the first time, I understood why I was struggling mentally, emotionally and physically and I began my journey to living a healthier and happier life.

Along this path I was introduced to a plethora of theories, techniques and practices. These enabled me to create new beliefs and healthier ways of thinking, feeling and coping. For the first time in my life I was in control; I wasn't drowning in negativity or being limited by anxiety. I was able to respond to situations, rather than react in old, unhelpful ways.

During the past 16 years, I've heard the words "But I should be fine" uttered by people from all walks of life. Over time it became clear; while each person had their own unique life story, like me, they too had a tendency to:

- Negatively overthink
- Feel overwhelmed or get stuck in feelings
- Live in an anxious state
- Put other people's needs first (people-please)
- Be consumed by self-doubt

Each of them wondered why they were suffering, despite no apparent trauma in their past. Interestingly, they also tended to have the same aha! moments in the counselling room. Aha! moments are those magical moments in counselling when new insight, awareness and understanding lead to relief, empowerment and change. Over the years I've witnessed many clients climb their way out of suffering, reclaiming their mental, emotional and physical health, ultimately changing their life.

I decided to write this book because I believe many of us suffer even when life seems to be going our way. I wanted to show why this is the case and, most importantly, share these aha! moments so others can also make the changes they need to live a healthier and happier life.

What you can expect from this book

By the end of this book you will:

- **Feel a huge sense of relief**. There are three main causes of most of us feeling far from fine, even when everything seems to be going our way. Normalising our human experience is super helpful, so prepare to feel a great weight lifted from your shoulders in chapter 1.
- **Gain bucketloads of awareness**. In chapters 2 to 6, you are going to get up close and personal with your beliefs, thoughts, feelings, body sensations and behaviours. I will help shine a light on what's working for you and pinpoint where you need to make some changes.
- **Feel empowered to take back control of your health and happiness**. Think of chapters 7 to 13 as your pocket guide for life. I will walk you through techniques and practices that will help you time and again. You will learn how to speak to yourself and coach yourself through whatever life throws at you. Whether it's an unexpected presentation or a worldwide pandemic, you will learn to respond to any situation without drowning in negativity or anxiety.

Throughout the book, you can expect the aha! moments to arrive through psychoeducation, moving and humorous stories, exercises, examples, fab practices, awesome techniques and, bizarrely but I hope you find rather effectively, the life of my dog. You will quickly learn I'm not a fan of psychobabble, much preferring to get the point across through a relatable story rather than clinical or dull jargon. Many of these stories are from my own personal life, my training and my experience of being counselled. While I seldom self-disclose when counselling a client, I have decided to do so in this book. I share my stories for two reasons: firstly, to aid your understanding and bring the subject to life; and secondly, to encourage you to step into your vulnerability and find your courage, by demonstrating mine.

How to use this book

I don't know about you but when I'm aware a book is crammed full with aha! moments, I am tempted to flick ahead to the bits I think I need. While I can't stop you doing this, I would encourage you to resist the temptation for one simple reason: lasting change starts with awareness. I know we have only just met but I'm asking you to trust me – and the process – and start at the beginning. In the first half of the book you will build up your awareness, slowly and deeply, to help sow seeds that will bloom into effective and long-lasting change. If you invest here, you will get the relief and change you desire when you work through the second half of the book.

Also, please take your time with this book. The content offers you an abundance of food for thought and includes many exercises, techniques and practices. It isn't a quick page-turner to get to the whodunnit at the end; it's a pick up, reflect, ponder and apply learning kind of book. Some of this you will be able to use straight away and other parts you may need to come back to when the time is right. As I said, think of it as a pocket guide for life, something you come back to as and when you need to.

To help you absorb as much as you can during your reading, I will be inviting you to reflect and complete some exercises. For those of you who want to go deeper, I suggest journaling at the same time. I will talk more about expressive writing later in the book, but journaling is a hugely effective way of reflecting and learning. You can write as much or as little as you like, and it doesn't have to be in a fancy notebook or in your best handwriting. Journaling helps me to extract those messy thoughts and feelings and put them in a safe place. The mere act of reflecting in my notebook always provides relief and enables me to make sense of new learnings. If journaling is not your cup of tea then could you set aside some thinking time to reflect and check in with your learnings? Even a little bit of quiet time in the shower or while walking the dog can get those awareness seeds fed and watered. You can start now ...

 Take some time here to think about how you can set yourself up to get the most out of all the aha! moments about to come your way.

How to apply the emergency brake

Before we start our journey together, I just need to be really clear that this book is not intended to replace counselling in any way, shape or form. It's here to help you gain more awareness of why you might be thinking, feeling and behaving in certain ways and to provide you with techniques, and practices, to help you change where you need to.

I also want you to know this might not all be plain sailing. You see, while gaining awareness is essential for change and ultimately for personal growth, it can also reveal some truths of which we were previously blissfully unaware. It's therefore inevitable that at times this book may bring up some uncomfortable thoughts, feelings and physical sensations. When this happens, you need to learn how to apply your emergency brake so you don't become overwhelmed.

The emergency brake analogy comes from my experience of learning to drive. I couldn't afford to learn until my early twenties, so when I had enough cash saved up, I booked myself onto an intensive course. After years of relying on buses, trains and my cheap-as-chips child's bike (one of the benefits of being 5ft tall) I was full of excitement about the endless possibilities from learning to drive. As I rocked up to my first four-hour intensive lesson, I was eager to put my foot down and just drive; thankfully, my much wiser instructor had different ideas. As soon as he taught me how to accelerate a little, he taught me how to brake a lot and made me practise over and over again until I knew it in my bones.

Essentially, my instructor taught me how to keep myself safe, and that's what you need to do when your brain is racing with thoughts and your body is gripped by uncomfortable feelings. To do this, I will teach you two simple ways of calming your brain and body. While these *are* simple, they aren't easy, because in order for them to work effectively you will need to practise. Braking in a car is technically simple, but my instructor made me do it lots of times to teach my brain and body how to respond sensibly rather than unhelpfully. The more you practise, the more you will respond healthily to an uncomfortable situation. So, without further ado, here are the emergency brake techniques I'd like you to practise.

Belly breathing

First up is breathing. I know you have been breathing all your life, but do you know how to breathe properly? Stick with me on this ...! Most people take shallow breaths into their chest and use only about a third of their lung capacity. Look down at your chest now. As you breathe naturally, what can you see rising? Is it your chest or your belly? When we breathe deeply into our belly, we engage our diaphragm, use our full lung capacity and take in more oxygen. This is super helpful because the additional oxygen sends a signal to our brain telling it we are safe. We can therefore use our breath like a brake to stop anxiety and other feelings overwhelming us.

Try it now by taking three deep breaths:

- Place your hand on your belly
- Breathe deep into your belly (not your chest) for a count of 5, feeling it gently push your hand outwards
- Breathe out for a count of 7, feeling your hand return
- Repeat two more times

It feels really good, doesn't it? This simple practice is fab for relaxing, so whenever you feel gripped by an uncomfortable feeling or by anxiety, try to take some long and deep belly breaths.

The 5-4-3-2-1 grounding technique

Next up is the 5-4-3-2-1 grounding technique. This may seem too simple to work but it slows down anxiety surges by distracting our brain. Anxiety flows where focus goes, so if we distract our senses with this simple technique then our brain thinks it's safe and reduces the anxiety hormones being released into our body.

- LOOK for 5 things you can see around you
  Examples: Notices on the wall; cars passing the window; pictures on your phone that make you smile

- TOUCH 4 things around you or on your body
  Examples: The soft material on your top; the fluffy cushion on the sofa; the thick socks on your feet; the smooth skin on your cheek

- LISTEN to 3 sounds around you
  Examples: A clock ticking; distant planes overhead; nature

- SMELL 2 things around you
  Examples: Your favourite perfume; your deodorant; the distant food smells wafting around

- TASTE 1 thing
  Examples: Remember the coffee you just had or pop a mint in your mouth and embrace the sensations

This simple technique can be used anytime, anywhere, so next time you need to bring a little calm, try this and see if it helps.

Throughout the book I will remind you of these calming techniques and introduce you to others. Now you know what to expect and how to look after yourself, buckle up and let's begin our journey.

CHAPTER 1

Why none of us are fine

It takes courage to live through suffering;
and it takes honesty to observe it.

CS LEWIS

In the 1980s my Mum would cook cheesy mashed potatoes with a side helping of Heinz baked beans, and I would lap it up. I mean what kid wouldn't like that carb and fat combination? The 1980s were an interesting time in Great Britain; it was the age of chicken supreme in a tin can, dodgy perms and of course iconic music. It was also the decade that saw the now infamous Live Aid concert, which raised much-needed funds for and awareness of the challenges in some parts of Africa. An unexpected side effect of this campaign was to remind all parents in good old GB of an ingenious way to motivate their children to eat their dinner. If for some reason I dared to leave some cheesy mash and baked beans, my Mum would screech "Eat your beans! There are starving kids in Africa". This phrase was echoed throughout the homes of Britain and had us eating every morsel on our plate like our future moral compass depended on it.

While most households have thankfully left this message back in the last century where it belongs, its undertones are still very much alive and kicking across many cultures in the world. The message is clear: "There are other people worse off than you so just get on with it." I detest this way of thinking with a passion because it leads people to make a crude comparison between their suffering and others' and conclude they should be fine. Now, while I am a big fan of practising gratitude, and having a rational view of our life, the idea we shouldn't be suffering because someone else is worse off than us is unhelpful to say the least. There isn't a finite amount of suffering to go around; suffering is suffering, and when we are in mental, emotional or physical pain, it doesn't mean others also in pain have to just get on with it. What actually helps us, and the people around us, is to honestly recognise and understand our own suffering. It is only when we let go of this harmful message that we can free ourselves to start this courageous journey.

 As I mentioned, I will be encouraging you to reflect at various points while reading the book, so grab your journal and a cuppa and take a few minutes to ponder the following questions:

- *Do you recognise the message that you shouldn't suffer because other people are worse off than you?*
- *Do you think you should be fine?*
- *Do you ever dismiss, compare or minimise your suffering?*

Bearing in mind what you have just read, will you give yourself permission today to stop comparing yourself with others? Making this commitment is important as it frees you from guilt and gives you a positive starting point for change.

When life gives you lemons

Before we move on to exploring the main reasons why many of us suffer, I want to explore the general idea of suffering a little more. Sometimes life throws us some really painful situations, which completely knock us off our feet. Grief, redundancy, health challenges and even things we didn't see coming, like pandemics or war. So let's be clear: to be fine and dandy in these situations is very difficult. When we face a deeply upsetting, traumatic or terrifying situation, it is natural for our mental, emotional and physical health to suffer. To deny the reality of this only damages our health even more. In these situations, we shouldn't be fine. However, we still very much have a choice about how we respond to the situation.

For example, I started writing this book before I'd ever heard the word coronavirus and now I find myself living through a pandemic. To pretend everything is fab is unrealistic. I, like many others in the world, am facing a huge amount of uncertainty and a real threat to life. I shouldn't be fine and I'm not. I don't have the brain power to use the time to learn a new language or skill. I don't have the energy or the emotional capacity to start a new business. However, what I do have a choice over is how I respond to the situation.

I can choose to create additional suffering by overthinking and creating heaps of unnecessary anxiety. I can choose to stuff my feelings down and numb them with carbs and wine. I can feed my anxious body with news, and I can put other people's needs before my own by saying yes to a video call when I really need to say no and rest. Then, to top it all off, at the end of each day I can beat myself up for not being 100% productive.

However, there is another option. I can choose to reduce my suffering by responding to the situation in a healthy way. I can decide not to catastrophise and instead think from a rational perspective. I can acknowledge the situation and be compassionate towards myself. I can express my feelings safely, give my body what it needs to rest and look after my needs as well as those of others.

The problem most of us have is that, even when life appears "normal" and we aren't facing a major threat, we find it difficult to respond healthily to bad situations. So, when life gives us lemons, instead of making lemonade, most of us are left with a sourness in our lives as we overthink, feel anxious, people-please and doubt ourselves.

During the course of studying this book you are going to learn how to help yourself in such situations rather than react unhealthily. Before we crack on with this, I want to tell you about three reasons why our health suffers during the good, the bad and the downright ugly times in life and why it's time to acknowledge them.

Introducing the Three Amigos

1. The survival brain
2. The should trap
3. The family blueprint

Before I expand on the Three Amigos, let me introduce you to my mischievous pooch, Paddy. He is a one-foot-tall, ginger Cavapoo and looks like a teddy bear. His hobbies include eating sausages, barking at squirrels and rolling in every single muddy puddle he can find. I'm not going to lie, there are days when I envy Paddy. There he sits, all curled up on our bed – which we obviously said we would never allow him to do – and I think I would love to be a dog. I mean life just seems so simple for him. He doesn't wake up and immediately feel a bolt of anxiety about his extensive to-do list: chase cat; bark at squirrel at least 50 times; go for a walk with my mates Ted and Alf, the Beagles. He doesn't spend ages thinking about whether he played fetch well enough yesterday or worrying about whether he is a good enough dog. Nope, he gets up, has his breakfast, goes into the garden to bark at the squirrels, comes back in for a cuddle and then promptly falls back to sleep. Sure, life's not all peachy; when he is out and about you can see him scanning for danger. Is that big Husky in the park today who has little regard for his personal space? Is a child going to appear out of nowhere and pull his tail again? Nope, life isn't all peachy, but he still seems a whole lot happier than most of us humans.

1. The survival brain

It will not be a shock to learn that while humans and dogs are both classed as mammals, we have evolved very differently. One thing we do have in common though is our survival instinct. Just like our furry friends, a part of our human brain is constantly scanning for danger. We do this because, in evolutional terms, it wasn't so long ago that our cave-dwelling ancestors spent their days foraging for food and keeping an eye out for those nasty sabre-toothed tigers. Unfortunately, even though sabre-toothed tigers are now extinct, and we can order takeaway from the comfort of our sofa, the survival part of our brain hasn't changed much. Its one and only job (then and now) is to keep us safe. While on the surface that seems like a noble cause, it actually creates a whole host of problems for us in modern-day life. This is because the survival brain finds it difficult to distinguish between a life-threatening situation (for example, being run over by a car) and a non-life-threatening situation (like accidentally sending a loving text message to your boss instead of your partner).

To make matters worse, the survival brain has a direct line to our body's panic button, so every time it perceives a threat, it floods us with anxiety. This is fantastic when it spots that car coming towards us as it saves our life, but it becomes super annoying when it goes off throughout the day each time we entertain the idea of going out of our comfort zone or when we make a mistake. Yep, that cavedweller in our head is responsible for those negative thoughts and much of our anxiety.

It may be reassuring to know that everyone has a version of this negative voice in their head. It takes on its very own personality as we grow up. It may be critical and judgemental, or a constant worrier, or both. It can even have its own gender identity. My inner voice is male, which is why I refer to it as my Inner Caveman, and that's the term I use throughout this book. In chapter 2 you are going to get up close and personal with your own Inner Caveman, but before that, let's look at the other Amigos that cause us to feel far from fine.

2. The should trap

The second reason why many of us suffer is that we get caught up in chasing our worth, which in dog equivalence is chasing our own tail. It amazes me that humans are so capable and yet sometimes we really don't help ourselves. We are far more intelligent than dogs; we can invent cool stuff like cars, can build ridiculously tall skyscrapers and can light a fire when we are cold, but we are plagued with self-doubt. This is where I really envy Paddy. For example, he is terrible at fetch because he refuses to bring the ball back. Does he sit and ponder this for ages? Does he think it makes him a failure or somehow less of a dog? Nope, he doesn't give it a second thought. Does he look in the mirror and tell himself he should be thinner or a stronger dog? Nope, he looks in the mirror and barks at himself because he thinks there is another dog in the room. And don't get me started on his total disregard for his education; he totally flunked puppy school because he was too busy playing with Hugo the Cockapoo to listen to the instructions. Does he get caught up in whether he should have passed or failed? Does he compare his intelligence with Badger the Schnauzer's? Nope, he doesn't care.

So, while dogs don't have a need to feel worthy, us humans do. Before we dig a little deeper into this, let me explain what I mean by worthy. I believe, at the most fundamental level, all humans are inherently worthy, and no one life is worth more, or less, than another. No matter your ethnicity, gender, sexuality, IQ or productivity levels on a rainy winter's morning in January, you are worthy just for being human.

If you struggle with this concept, think about when a baby makes its way into the world. Is your first thought that it's worthless because it can't go out and earn its keep yet? Of course not; even if we aren't huge baby fans, we recognise our deep human connection to this little bundle of endless screaming joy and wouldn't dream of questioning its worth.

When humans respect this inherent worth then beautiful things happen; children flourish in unconditional love, adults feel validated and people come together in the big moments and small moments in life. Unfortunately, us humans seem to have lost our way and have created a world where we are all surrounded by messages that put conditions on our worth. Every day we see, and hear, messages from family, friends or strangers telling us who we should be and what we should be doing and judging our worth when we don't live up to their expectations.

As if this wasn't enough, we also have these messages pelted at us from all angles, from the media to our educational and political systems. Conditions of worth have infested our everyday life and, all over the world, people are crippled by self-doubt.

These messages are often communicated using the word *should*. If there is one word I hate most in the English language, it's *should*. Never has a word brought so much doom and gloom to a person's face than when they say it. Seriously, try saying any of these common should statements and see how it affects your mood:

- I should be fine, as other people have it much worse than me
- I should be more successful
- I should be more productive
- I should be a proper adult by now
- I should be thin

We suffer because, when we hear a message like "You should be thin" we internalise this as "*I* should be thin, and I will be worthy when I *am* thin". We then get caught up in trying really hard to lose weight but find we still don't feel worthy when we do. Unfortunately, rather than taking a step back and owning our inherent worth, we continue the pattern and try to do something else we are told we should do, only to realise that doesn't make us feel worthy either. We get caught up chasing our elusive WoW factors – the things we believe are going to make us feel worthy. However, they never do.

The WoW here stands for Web of Worth. We become so caught up in chasing our worth that we can't see we are stuck in an elaborate web of conditions of worth, spun by the people and very powerful systems around us. We become trapped in a vicious circle, trying to prove ourselves, and all it brings is exhaustion, pain, anxiety and perpetual self-doubt.

3. The family blueprint

Last, but by no means least, we have the final reason why none of us are fine: our upbringing, or family blueprint as I like to call it. Now I'm not here to pick your upbringing apart. This is not that book. This book is all about empowering you to move from suffering to mental, emotional and physical health and happiness. Understanding why you have suffered is an important part of the journey.

I personally believe parenting is the hardest job in the world, and the vast majority of people are doing their best.

Paddy's dog mum had it easy: feed Paddy and his six siblings, teach them how to pee away from the sleeping area and get them to play nicely. However, our human needs are far more complex, meaning our parenting is a lot more challenging.

There are lots of theories about human needs, most notable being Maslow's Hierarchy of Needs, so feel free to do a little research on this topic. I prefer to simplify it down to these 10 needs:

1. **Physical health**: Our body's need to function. We all need to sleep, hydrate, breathe, pee, move, rest and, of course, eat (h-anger is a real thing, people!).
2. **Safety**: Our need to be safe, secure and protected.
3. **Mental health**: Our need to have rational beliefs, realistic thoughts and perspective.
4. **Emotional health**: Our need to identify and express our feelings safely.
5. **Love and connection**: Our need to connect with others, be loved and belong.
6. **Worth**: Our need to be seen and heard, to feel valued, significant and validated.
7. **Spiritual**: Our need to follow our faith (if it is part of our belief system).
8. **Growth**: Our need to learn, adapt and develop.
9. **Cultural**: Our need to follow cultural practices.
10. **Financial**: Our need to provide resources for our other needs; we all need dosh to pay for stuff.

I don't know about you but I find looking after my own needs a daily challenge, so having to take responsibility for a child's too is always going to be a struggle at times. To make it even harder, not only have most parents inherited an outdated "How to Parent" guide from their family, but they also have that Inner Caveman running riot in their heads while simultaneously chasing their own worth. Unfortunately, children learn by watching, listening and repeating, so if a parent overthinks or worries, suppresses their feelings, suffers from anxiety, says yes even when they need to say no and doubts themselves then we learn to do that too.

Our family blueprint also leads us to form one of the most important beliefs we have as humans: whether our needs matter or not. As children, if our needs were not met, we may form the belief that our needs don't matter, and we may find ourselves always putting other people's needs first as a result. This can lead us to people-please our way through life, and this behaviour, as you will discover later, is very costly to our mental, emotional and physical health. Yep, parenting is definitely the hardest job in the world, and how our needs were met as a child feeds into how we meet our own needs as an adult.

What happened to me?

There was a time when I used to beat myself up for feeling far from fine. I just didn't understand why I couldn't get a grip. When I became angry with myself my head would scream "What's wrong with me?" This question was never helpful and always left my brain spiralling through a litany of negative thoughts.

Turns out many of us are familiar with this question. If this has ever looped around your brain for more than a few minutes, then I'm willing to bet the answer you found within yourself was:

- Unkind
- Unhelpful
- Untrue

The question I, and my clients, have found more helpful to ask is "*What happened to me?*" This takes away the need to beat ourselves up and stops us falling into that rabbit hole of negativity. Instead, it encourages us to explore and understand some of the underlying reasons why we all – you, me and your next-door neighbour – suffer at times. This understanding not only lifts a great weight from our shoulders, but it also frees us to start the journey of taking back control. So, let's start answering this question by exploring how the Three Amigos have shown up in your life to date.

Your survival brain (aka Inner Caveman)

Think of it like this: your survival brain is the first part of your brain to respond to any situation, and it hasn't updated its "How to Keep a Human Safe" plan for thousands of years. This means that since birth you've had a caveman running around in your head trying to navigate its way through the modern world with its outdated five golden rules:

1. There is no room for compassion. Compassion does not help you outrun a sabre-toothed tiger.
2. Standing out or being on your own is dangerous (see previous issue with sabre-toothed tiger). Fitting into a tribe is the best way to keep safe, get fed and get watered.
3. Treat every situation, and person, as a potential threat, so constantly scan for danger.
4. Minimise uncertainty, maximise certainty.
5. Learn from dangerous near misses (such as sabre-toothed tiger incidents or rival tribe fights) and ruminate on the situation so it can be stored as a survival technique.

In modern daily life, your Inner Caveman's outdated voice appears like this:

1. Being kind and compassionate to yourself does not keep you safe. Therefore, this voice is often blunt and sometimes downright rude.
2. As it's dangerous to stand out, it tries to talk you out of doing scary things – like giving a presentation in front of 50 staring strangers, or setting up that company – by telling you that you are going to make a fool of yourself. As it believes it's much safer to fit in, it tries to sabotage that promotion by declaring you don't know enough. It keeps you out of the

limelight by filling you with imposter thoughts, and it likes to compare you with others in the tribe so you can keep up.

3. It sees everything as negative. It worries about everything, from what others think, to whether you have left the iron on.

4. It will avoid, overplan or fill you with anxiety when faced with uncertainty. From an unexpected phone call, to a pandemic coming out of nowhere and messing up your daily plans, your Inner Caveman hates uncertainty with a passion and doesn't mind telling you.

5. It overthinks, and it ruminates about mistakes, situations, conversations and more (especially in the middle of the night).

As I said earlier, while our Inner Cavemen all follow these rules, they each develop their own unique personality based on our upbringing and life experiences. For some, the voice develops into a mouse-like whisper, but for many others it's a screaming monkey.

My Inner Caveman is called Brian and he is The Comfort Zone King who lives inside my head. I'm aware that sounds a little strange, but bear with me. You see, Brian loves it when I'm safely in my comfort zone, and who can blame him, eh? Our comfort zones can often be warm, snuggly places, full of safety and certainty. Whether I am under a blanket on a cold winter's day or emotionally tucked away from the world, Brian knows how to keep me safe, and there are times when I blooming love Brian for it.

However, there are also times when Brian can be, let's just say, a little on the controlling side. He gets so focused on me being safe in my comfort zone that he will resort to anything to keep me there. He tempts me to avoid situations or pumps me with so much anxiety I don't want to do them anyway. He holds me back by comparing me with others and calling me an imposter. He worries about, well, everything really, to the point where my thoughts go around and around. He is super pessimistic and tries to convince me I've left the front door unlocked each time I leave the house, and let's not forget his rather mean side that berates me for even the smallest of mistakes.

 In chapter 2 you are going to get up close and personal with your own Inner Caveman. For now, can you recognise how these outdated rules have been influencing the way you think, feel and behave? Grab your journal, a coffee and a biscuit and mull over these questions:

- *Does your inner voice lack compassion and kindness?*
- *Have you been known to avoid things like public speaking?*
- *Do you think you're an imposter?*
- *Do you compare yourself with others?*
- *Do you have a tendency to over-worry?*
- *How do you feel when faced with uncertainty?*
- *Do you ruminate over conversations, mistakes or situations?*

As you can see, the survival part of our brain is responsible for much of our negative thinking, self-doubt and anxiety. With this voice in our head, is it any wonder so many of us find ourselves suffering?

Your shoulds and WoW factors

Growing up I received some very direct messages about who I should be and what I should, and shouldn't, be doing. For example, when I wanted to study Psychology at A level I was told in no uncertain terms that it wasn't a proper subject and I wouldn't be able to get a proper job, so I should do a pure subject like Maths instead. Other messages were a bit subtler, like all the thin, feminine girls and women on the front of every single magazine I bought in the 1980s and 1990s. They didn't tell me I should be thin and feminine, but they implied it with their lack of diversity. Then there were the messages that were communicated with a look of disgust or a comment. Every time a gay person was on the TV in our house, there was a tut, and a look of disgust, communicating that difference was not allowed. Here are some of the messages I received about who I should be, and what I should be doing, as a child. As you read through these, do any sound familiar?

Family system:
- You should get top grades
- You should be feminine
- You should study pure subjects
- You should go to university

27

- You should be heterosexual
- You should do better
- You should be perfect

Education system:
- You should be in top sets
- You should get top grades
- You should go to university, or you will end up working in a supermarket

Culture system:
- Women should be perfect
- Women should be feminine
- Women should be thin
- You should be in a relationship
- You should be heterosexual
- You should have children

Media system:
- You should be feminine
- You should be thin
- You should be pretty
- You should wear make-up
- You should be popular

As these messages came from influential people and the powerful systems around me, I had no reason to doubt their validity, and I therefore put all my energy into following them. This is how, at the tender age of 22, I came to be staring up at Canary Wharf on one cold September morning in 2000. Having graduated from university with a Maths degree (it's a pure subject, people), I had landed myself a fancy job on the 35th floor of the UK's tallest building. I was, from that day onwards, going to be a commercial underwriter. I had little idea what a commercial underwriter actually did, and had no childhood dream of working in insurance but, as I stood there in my Dorothy Perkins suit, I was pretty sure I had made it. I had done everything I should; I had followed the world's recipe for success, I officially had a proper job and, dare I say it, I felt like a proper adult.

However, as each day, week and then year came to pass, I became painfully aware that I was not being rewarded as promised; actually, quite the contrary. I still didn't feel worthy; in fact, my self-worth had more holes in it than a block of Swiss cheese, all the time chasing the next WoW factor (the thing I thought was going to make me feel worthy) and forever feeling not good enough. I was stuck in a never-ending loop of seeking validation from others and, most painfully of all, I had lost sight of who I truly was. I was anxious, full of shame and lost. Ouch.

If my story sounds familiar to you then fear not, because throughout the course of this book I will be helping you break free from the should trap.

However, before you can do this you need to become acquainted with the should messages in your life.

Exercise: Are you shoulding all over yourself?

I'm aware the term shoulding all over yourself isn't particularly pleasant, but I'm hoping it will stick in your memory enough to remember why it's so important not to get caught up in the should trap. Before you begin, I want you to take three deep belly breaths to ease yourself into this exercise.

When you feel ready, take some time to review the following list and start to mull over those should messages you received, and still receive, from:

- Family
- Friends
- Peers
- Culture
- Society
- Media: News and social media
- Education institutions
- Religious organisations

Grab a piece of paper, and some pens, and draw a capital **I** and fill it with all the should messages that you have internalised.

If you need a little inspiration, here is my **I**.

Now it's your turn. I should ... Remember to take your time with this exercise. Set it aside and apply an emergency brake if you need to.

When you have completed this, I want you to highlight the shoulds that have become your WoW factors. By this I mean the shoulds that affect your sense of worth, such as where you think "I should be thin and I will be worthy when I'm thin".

When I worked through this exercise, I was shocked, not only by the sheer volume of messages being pelted at me, but also by how I had internalised them and made many into my WoW factors. I desperately wanted to feel worthy and good enough. I thought that becoming who I *should* be and doing what I *should* do was the answer. I was stuck in my very own Web of Worth. Although this exercise was uncomfortable at times, it really helped me to understand why I had suffered for so long and it motivated me to make the changes I needed to break free.

 As you work through the book I will help you to let go of those troublesome should messages and free yourself from your Web of Worth. For now, take some time to reflect on your experience of this exercise in your journal. It's not uncommon for this to raise different feelings, so don't forget to apply your emergency brake if you need to.

Your family blueprint

I was brought up in the West Midlands in the 1980s and 1990s. My parents worked hard, just like theirs before them, to put cheesy mashed potato on the table and a roof over my head. My safety and physiological needs were met most of the time, but needs like mental and emotional health and my need to feel worthy were just not in their realm of awareness. This meant they couldn't help themselves, let alone me. Looking back on those times, there was a lot of fear, shame and anxiety flowing around our house. They hadn't been taught by their folks how to understand or express their feelings, so how were they supposed to model this to me? Similarly, they would overthink and over-worry but, again, how were they supposed to know how damaging this was to me when they didn't know themselves?

How your needs were attended to as a child will have influenced the way you think, feel and behave and will have led you to form a belief around whether your needs matter or not. To help you gain more awareness of your family blueprint, take some time to ponder over the following questions about your parents, guardians or whoever brought you up.

A little word of warning first though. Please remember we aren't here to judge or blame your folks for what they did and didn't do. If you do find yourself becoming upset or angry then use your emergency stop and take a break.

Mental health needs:
• Did your parents worry a lot or overthink?
• Did they ever talk to you about mental health?

Emotional needs:
- Could your parents express their feelings safely?
- Were you encouraged to talk about your feelings and did you feel safe doing this with them?

Physical needs:
- Were your parents anxious and on the go all the time?
- Could they prioritise self-care?
- How were your physical needs nurtured?

Worth needs:
- Did your parents show signs of self-doubt?
- Did you feel seen and validated by them?

General:
Lastly, how did your parents look after their needs in general?
- Did they put other people's needs before their own and people-please?
- Did they make you feel like other people's needs mattered more than yours?

How did you find those questions? If you found it uncomfortable or aren't sure about the answers then don't force it. You are merely at the start of this journey so just let the questions percolate for a bit and see what comes up for you.

Remember, this isn't about blame but about recognising how you learned about meeting your needs. The good news is you may not have had much control of your situation as a child but, as an adult, you can learn new ways of meeting your needs, and this book will help you do this.

The Infamous Five

As we become acquainted with the Three Amigos, it often quickly becomes clear why many of us suffer. However, it also explains how we suffer. As I mentioned in the introduction, many people suffer with the following five issues. While trauma and life experiences can cause these issues, in many people they are thanks to the Three Amigos. Let's recap on the Infamous Five:

1. **A noisy, negative voice in your head**: Some call it overthinking or constant worrying. Often critical, seldom kind, it's like a negative soundtrack stuck on repeat.
2. **Feeling overwhelmed at times**: While the severity of this may ebb and flow, many of the feelings linger like a bad smell.
3. **Feeling anxious**: The body finds it difficult to be in a calm state.
4. **Stuck in people-pleasing behaviours**: For example, saying yes when really needing to say no, and avoiding conflict.
5. **Consumed with pesky self-doubt**: Doubting your own abilities, believing you are an imposter or not good enough and often seeking validation from others.

Your superhuman powers

Congratulations! If the five issues resonated with you to some extent then you are normal. Okay, I'm not a fan of the word normal, so let's go with typical. This life malarkey is tough, and we all have an annoying Inner Caveman, a set of complicated should messages and a wonky family blueprint to contend with. That means none of us are set up to be fine in life, so the important question is can we be fine or, even better, can we be more than fine? The answer to this is a resounding yes.

You see, humans are an incredible species like no other. Admittedly, we get off to a slow start compared with some other species. Yes, Paddy could ring a bell to go outside to the toilet within 10 weeks, and it takes us a lot longer, but once we get going our development knows no bounds.

We have much more advanced abilities than other mammals; for example, we have a more sophisticated brain, which allows us to think beyond the negative. This means we can bring our Inner Caveman under control and help it develop into more of a glass half full rational kind of guy than a pessimistic everything is terrible kind of guy.

We are also the kings and queens of gaining awareness and of using this to adapt in order to help ourselves. We can turn our self-doubt into self-clout and override our old patterns of behaviours, leading us to take assertive action rather than people-pleasing. Lastly, we can grow and learn new ways of expressing our feelings and overcoming our anxiety.

The fact is, you have the ability to overcome all Infamous Five issues. You just don't know how to do this yet, but this is why you are reading this book.

Now, as much as I would love to advance straight to the "and this is how to change" bit, we need to get more acquainted with all five issues and, specifically, how they show up in your life. I know it's tempting to jump ahead, but this exploration is super important because, unless you know how to spot these sneaky so-and-sos, you won't be able to stop them.

In the next five chapters, we are going to explore each of these issues in detail and I will help you become aware of how these ways of thinking, feeling and behaving wiggle their way into your everyday life. Once you have gained oodles of insight and awareness in these chapters, you will then move on to learning techniques and practices that will help you overcome these issues and take back control of your health and happiness levels.

Right now, though, take some time to read through the summary, grab a journal and reflect on what you learned about yourself in this chapter. Remember you aren't looking to cast blame or get stuck in the past; you are looking to learn about yourself so you can move forward.

Therefore, if this reflection brings up too many feelings or leads to looping thoughts, step away and apply your emergency brake and then come back to this later.

Key aha! moments

Congratulations, you have completed chapter 1. It has been jam-packed with wisdom, so here are the key aha! moments for you to refer back to, as and when you need a little reminder.

1. We often compare our suffering with that of others and wrongly conclude that we should be fine. All humans suffer to some extent during their lives and ignoring the pain or telling ourselves to just get on with it helps no one.
2. Sometimes life gives us lemons and we naturally suffer. However, we have the power to make our suffering worse or better depending on how we respond to the situation.
3. "What happened to me?" is a much healthier question to ask than "What's wrong with me?"
4. There are three reasons why none of us are fine even in the best of times, aka the Three Amigos:
   - Our survival brain hasn't evolved since our cave-dwelling days and causes complete chaos
   - We get trapped in the many should messages we hear and we suffer when we chase our worth as a result

- Our family blueprint influences how we think, express our feelings and cope, and it also leads us to form beliefs around whether our needs matter or not

5. Many people suffer with the following five issues as a result of the Three Amigos:
   - A noisy negative voice
   - Feeling overwhelmed
   - Feeling anxious
   - Stuck in people-pleasing behaviours
   - Consumed with pesky self-doubt

6. Humans are mammals with superpowers; we have the ability to gain awareness, adapt and grow. This means we can overcome these issues and take back control of our life.

CHAPTER 2

Your Inner Caveman

It's not what you say out of your mouth that determines your life,
it's what you whisper to yourself that has the most power.

ROBERT KIYOSAKI

Brian, my Inner Caveman, began to make himself known as a vague whisper in my early childhood. Like many, Brian started out by mimicking how the adults in my life spoke to me, and he certainly learned quickly. It started with the classic bullying behaviour of name-calling. Yes, labelling myself an idiot was part of a daily ritual for me. From getting my spelling wrong at school, to taking a telephone number down incorrectly, to dropping a plate, Brian saw these as evidence that I was an idiot, and he was more than happy to tell me.

Then, in my teens, the grump started to get demanding. He was tuning into the many "You should be X" and "You should be doing Y" messages around me and decided tough love was the ideal way to motivate a 13-year-old girl: "You should be thin"; "You should be popular"; "You should be getting A grades". When, of course, I couldn't meet these ridiculous demands, he went into ultra-critical mode.

By the time I popped out of education and into the big wide world in my twenties, Brian had got way too big for his boots. Like a broken record stuck on repeat, he would go over the never-ending list of what I should be doing and seemed to take delight in comparing me with others and calling me a failure as a result. When I did do something well, he downplayed it, saying I only got a good review because my line manager felt sorry for me or because I was lucky. Sure, Brian, I only got the job at Canary Wharf because I was lucky. Nothing to do with the blood, sweat and tears spent getting my Maths degree or the effort I put into the interview. Of course, I didn't say that to him at the time as I thought that's just how people spoke to themselves.

Brian's other really annoying habit was over-worrying. Not just every time I deemed to step out of my comfort zone but also about ridiculous things like "Did I lock the front door?" or "Did I leave the iron on?" His ability to overthink everything, from the household appliances burning the house down to the conversation I had with Jane three years ago, was staggering. Brian was noisy, relentless and dangerous, because I believed every single word.

Over the years, I've met many Inner Cavemen, and I've learned there are very few people who would speak to others as they do to themselves. From the covert, constant niggling whispers of doom to overt, full-blown bullies, these terrors live inside our head and are the cause of much suffering. It's the negative voice that never shuts up, providing a running commentary on our every waking moment. It's the voice that whips up a multitude of feelings; it's the voice that fills us with anxiety. Most importantly, it's the voice that notices we are struggling and declares "But I should be fine. I just need to get on with it."

10 tell-tale signs of a noisy Inner Caveman

Some people refer to their negative voice as overthinking or worrying, while others call it their Inner Critic. While these voices follow the same survival rules, they develop their own unique personality because of our different upbringing and life experiences. However, when we look closely, we often see that our voices share similar traits:

1. **Label loving**: calling yourself a name, such as idiot, bad, silly, stupid; it's never a positive label.
2. Worrying what everyone thinks and **mind reading**: thinking you know what people are thinking about you, and again it's never positive.
3. **Catastrophising**: about appliances burning the house down or other worst-case scenarios.
4. **Shoulds**: repeating those messages that you should be X, Y and of course Z, without pausing to decide if they are right for you.
5. **Imposter syndrome**: telling yourself you're a phoney and will be found out.

6. Grumpy **overgeneralising** about how everything is terrible.
7. **Discounting** and minimising anything positive you do and dismissing compliments.
8. **Comparing** yourself with everyone and their dog (okay, not the dog, but you get the point).
9. Playing the dodgy **fortune-telling** game of "What if ...?" (What if this happens? What if that happens?)
10. **Looping**, repetitive thoughts that go around and around.

 Did you find yourself nodding along to any of these signs? If so, are you aware of who may have taught you this way of thinking? Remember you aren't looking to blame anyone around you for modelling this way of thinking but just looking to understand more about yourself.

Why do we have an Inner Caveman?

As I mentioned in chapter 1, the Inner Caveman lives in the survival part of our brain, which has first dibs on responding to a situation. As that part of our brain hasn't evolved since our cave-dwelling days, we each have a negative voice that adheres to an outdated set of safety rules. This voice then develops its own unique personality based on our upbringing and life experiences.

Some people may find their Inner Caveman is more of an Inner Critic. It internalises all the should messages around them and berates them when they don't live up to those ridiculous expectations. For instance, if it heard "You should be successful" it repeats it over and over again, eggs the person on to engage in unhealthy behaviours, like working a 16-hour day, seven days a week, and then berates them for every little mistake made. It can be relentless and painful.

Our inner negative voices also differ because they listen to and learn from the people we grew up around. Like I said before, parenting is the hardest job in the world, and nobody wants to pass on their Inner Caveman. However, we all learn by watching and absorbing from those around us; the good, the bad and the ugly. This means if members of your immediate family over-worry or get bogged down in negative thoughts then you may have learned to do this too.

Lastly, our life experiences can greatly influence how we think. Our Inner Cavemen are here to keep us safe at all costs so, if we have experienced something traumatic, scary, upsetting or painful, it remembers and will do anything to stop us repeating this experience. This can lead to avoidance, numbing or over-checking behaviours.

The cost of listening to the Inner Caveman

For me, 30 years buying into the lies of my Inner Caveman took its toll. The noisy name-calling, and its ability to point out my failings on a daily basis, pumped me full of shame and left my self-worth in tatters. The over-worrying filled me with fear and kept the anxiety flowing through my body morning, noon and night, leading to sleepless nights and migraines. The never-ending should messages also encouraged me to engage in unhealthy behaviours. For instance, when I was 16 I revised relentlessly for months, and during my twenties I worked very long hours, saying yes to everything, even though it was clear I was overwhelmed.

From the outside, people may not have noticed I was far from fine. I was very good at looking like I was functioning, but on the inside I was suffering. Like any human, I had to form some coping mechanisms so I chose the not overly helpful option of avoidance by numbing with beer and comforting with carbs. While these helped numb those feelings in the moment, that just gave my Inner Caveman something else to chastise me for: "I should be a size 8. I shouldn't be eating chocolate!"

It's pretty obvious that the Inner Caveman can create a world of pain, but does it have any redeeming qualities? Well, yes ... but really no. Let me explain. The most common reasons I hear for people staying in an abusive relationship with their Inner Caveman are:

- Tough love gets results
- It helps me keep high standards
- It keeps me motivated by kicking me into action

Look, I totally get it. My teenage self did get mostly As, and my 20-plus self received great feedback at work; but it was because I bullied myself into achievement. I may have got the grades, but I couldn't enjoy them because they came with buckets of anxiety and constant self-doubt. The moral of the story is that you can't beat yourself to do something without beating yourself up in the process.

How to recognise your Inner Caveman

Now it's time to get up close and personal with your own Inner Caveman. To do this, I invite you to work your way through the following three exercises. Take your time with these and feel free to get creative.

Exercise 1: Name your Inner Caveman

I know this might seem a bit daft, but it's extremely helpful, because naming the voice helps provide some distance between you and it. You can make up a name or even call it after a cartoon or TV character.

If that doesn't work for you, do you want to stick with Inner Caveman or Inner Cavewoman? Does Inner Critic or negative voice work instead? Remember, whatever you decide, there is no right or wrong answer.

Exercise 2: Describe your Inner Caveman

Next up, how would you describe your Inner Caveman? Take a moment to visualise it and answer these questions:

- What does it look like? Is it an animal or cartoon character or human, or something else?
- What does it sound like?
- How would you describe its personality?

For example, here's mine:
- Brian is a cartoon tortoise. He is green and wears a crown because he thinks he is The Comfort Zone King.
- He speaks in a slow, grumpy tone but can turn into a vicious little git when he is at his critical worst.
- He worries a lot and is famous for jumping to the worst-case scenario and frightening the bejeezus out of me. He likes to criticise a lot, compares me with others and generally puts me down.

Again, I'm aware I may sound a little odd describing a tortoise that lives inside my head, but visualising the inner voice, and its attributes, will help you to recognise it from a mile off. After all, you can't stop it unless you learn how to spot it.

You know those moments in life when something suddenly clicks and you see something differently? Well, many years ago, while training to be a counsellor, I had one of those moments.

We were exploring cognitive behavioural therapy, or CBT as it is widely known, and we were introduced to a list of our brain's unhelpful thought types. As I read down the list, it was like someone had literally been listening inside my brain for years. Not only was it a huge relief to find out other people had a similar voice in their heads, but it was also instrumental in helping me recognise Brian.

In order to get to know your Inner Caveman even better you are shortly going to do an exercise to identify its favourite types of unhelpful thoughts. To help you, I will first run through the nine most common unhelpful thought types along with some examples. As you read through the list, pay attention to the ones that really resonate with you.

Unhelpful thought type 1: Labelling

Examples:
- I made a mistake; I'm an idiot
- I missed the deadline; I'm so stupid
- I didn't go for the job; I'm such a coward

Calling us names can be a daily ritual for many Inner Cavemen. It's like having a playground bully in your head.

Unhelpful thought type 2: Mind reading

Examples:
- Gina from accounts thinks I'm useless at my job
- Bob thinks I'm stupid
- Mel doesn't like me

I personally think this is the most impressive thought type as people believe they can actually mind read. Seriously, could you imagine the chaos if any of us could do this? What humans are good at, though, is projecting what we think about ourselves onto other people. If we think we are useless at our job and Gina from accounts doesn't say hello to us in the lift, we can easily think Gina from accounts thinks we are useless at our job. Nope, Gina from accounts woke at 2am because little Jonny couldn't sleep and she is more concerned with getting a triple espresso than saying hello to you.

Unhelpful thought type 3: Catastrophising

Examples:
- I'm late; I'm going to get fired
- Did I leave the iron on? It's going to burn the house down
- John hasn't texted, and he should have been at work 20 minutes ago (visualises John being in an accident)

All humans have the capacity to take a few bits of information and turn them into a catastrophe in the blink of an eye. Some people leap in a few seconds from making one mistake to being jobless and homeless, while others leap from leaving an iron on to burning down the entire street. These worst-case scenarios are incredibly unlikely, yet we can get so caught up in the thought it scares the bejeezus out of us.

Unhelpful thought type 4: Shoulds

Examples:
- I should be a size 8
- I should be perfect
- I should be productive all the time

Remember those should messages we explored in chapter 1? Well, your Inner Caveman is responsible for internalising these. I refer to this as "shoulding all over yourself" because, when you have an attack of the shoulds, you get caught up in chasing your worth and put yourself under extreme pressure.

Unhelpful thought type 5: Phoneyism

Examples:
- I'm an imposter
- I'm going to be found out
- I don't know enough

Congratulations, you have been promoted. You have poured blood, sweat and tears into getting this promotion, you celebrated in style all weekend and then, on Monday morning, this happens:
- Inner Caveman: What am I doing? I don't know enough. Who do I think I am? Why did I go for the promotion? They are going to find out I'm a fraud; I'm an imposter!

Phoneyism and imposter syndrome are very common in humans, from CEOs to actors, to counsellors and coaches and even Michelle Obama. In December 2018 every media outlet carried the news that Michelle Obama still felt like a fraud. She is quoted as saying "It doesn't go away, that feeling that you shouldn't take me that seriously." If the former First Lady feels like a fraud, then it's no wonder that sometimes we do too.

Unhelpful thought type 6: Overgeneralising

Examples:
- Everything in the world is terrible
- You can't trust anyone
- Nothing works out for me

Our Inner Caveman's recipe for overgeneralising is ...
- Take a few nights of crappy sleep
- Throw in a snotty cold
- Add a bunch of delayed trains (What do you mean leaves on the line?!)
- Drop some coffee down your new top

Et voila! You have created overgeneralising. "Everything is terrible; nothing works out for me!" becomes your mantra. It's super easy for our Inner Caveman to create this, but thankfully it's easy to stop once we have a rant about the trains and a good night's sleep. However, we have to be careful that this unhelpful thought doesn't fester because, when it does, it snowballs in our brain and becomes our general perspective.

Unhelpful thought type 7: Comparison

Examples:
- My sister is prettier than me
- Emma has 2000 followers, and I only have 200
- Dean is more successful than me

Comparison steals our happiness. For example, you are having a great day; you slept well last night, you got a free coffee on the way to work, you hit the gym at lunchtime (and are feeling super smug as a result), and you aced your meeting with Deepak. All is well in the world until you spot Susie from HR, who seems to be wearing the same top you bought at the weekend.

Enter Inner Caveman:
"Is that the top I bought on Saturday? Oh god, she looks loads better in it than me. Why can't I be as tall as Susie? She is so pretty, no wonder she has a boyfriend and I don't. I don't know why I bother going to the gym."

From happy to unhappy in two seconds. Thanks, Inner Caveman.

Unhelpful thought type 8: Discounting the positive

Examples:
- I only got 90% because the test was easy
- I only got the job because my friend works here
- I only got a good appraisal because she felt sorry for me

Welcome to discounting the positive. This is when we block out the good stuff.

Inner Caveman:
"I only got the job because no one else applied for it."

Nope. You got the job because you have lots of skills and experience, and you showed all those great traits in the interview.

Unhelpful thought type 9: The "What if ...?" game

Examples:

- What if I miss my train and I have to buy another ticket and then I won't have enough money to pay Simon back. What if Simon can't pay his rent this month, and what if he hates me?
- What if my Mum catches coronavirus? What if it affects her lungs? What if she goes into hospital, and what if I never see her again?

Last but not least we have the "What if ...?" game. At the start of the coronavirus pandemic in 2020, my Mum was identified as extremely clinically vulnerable because of her underlying health issues. When she displayed a few symptoms, Brian wanted to play the "What if...?" game. If I had let him play I would have been so full of anxiety I would have found it difficult to function. Even in much simpler times, this way of thinking can create a lot of anxiety, so we really need to watch out for this.

Exercise 3: Identify your Inner Caveman's favourite unhelpful thought types

Now you have read through the nine unhelpful thoughts, use what you've read to identify your own Inner Caveman's top three most prevalent types and jot down a few examples.

As with all the exercises, I am not going to ask you to do something I'm not willing to do myself, so here are Brian's top three types along with an example for each:

Labelling

Example:
Every time I made a mistake, did something wrong, got a low grade or otherwise messed up, Brian would call me an idiot. I must have let him do it at least 10 times a day.

Mind reading

Example:
Brian used to do this one all the time: she thinks this about me; he thinks that about me. For example, one day in my previous life (remember I used to work in a city job) I was in a meeting with Wendy, and she was, let's just say, a little on the touchy side. She had a face like thunder, clearly angry, and was unhappy about the progress of the project. After the meeting I thought "She hates me, she has always hated me, she thinks I'm rubbish at my job, and she wants me out". Twenty

minutes later she dropped by my desk, apologised for her behaviour and explained her Mum was ill and she was really worried. Turned out my mind-reading skills were way off track.

Catastrophising

Example:
If there was a Worrying Olympics, Brian would win gold for his ability to catastrophise in three seconds flat. One of his most spectacular moments was when I was flying to the US, about to embark on an epic adventure, and shortly after we landed he started to wonder if I had left the front door open. In three seconds, I went from merely wondering to visualising two robbers emptying the house, hearing the woman from the insurance company saying they wouldn't pay out and my other half leaving me for my sheer stupidity.

My top tip for testing a relationship is to turn to your other half after a 10-hour flight and declare "I think I've left the front door open". Even my wife, who was well used to the daily "Did I leave the straighteners on?" question, found this one a little bit difficult to respond to with loving reassurance.

Before we jump into our first awareness challenge, pause for a moment to reflect on how you found this exercise. Sometimes when we are learning about our brain, we can have eureka moments

like "Oh, I get it now! It makes so much sense", or moments when we feel overwhelmed and think "Oh, I do all of these, it's too much". If it's the former with you, great. But if it's the latter, take some time to settle with belly breaths or try the 5-4-3-2-1 grounding technique you experimented with in the introduction.

Remember, for the moment, all I am inviting you to do is reflect on the different types of thoughts. The initial chapters are all about growing your awareness, and I promise later in the book I will help you to make the changes you need. For now, though, take some time to digest the information you have learned. Use your journal, grab a cup of tea and talk it over with a trusted friend or take a well-earned break.

Awareness challenge

In chapter 8 you are going to learn how to hush your Inner Caveman and amplify your healthier voice, the Inner Coach. Don't worry, this doesn't mean lowering your standards or giving you an excuse to let yourself off the hook every time you don't go to the gym. The Inner Coach promotes growth and development, but it does it without leaving you covered in bruises. Before you learn to engage your Inner Coach you need to become even more familiar with your Inner Caveman. Remember, unless you can spot it, you won't be able to stop it.

Awareness really is the key to change; the more time you spend understanding your beliefs, thoughts, feelings, body sensations and behaviours the easier it is to change them. This is where the trusty awareness challenge comes to the fore. The aim of this exercise is to build on the awareness you have already gained from this chapter and apply it to your daily life.

I'll be inviting you to engage in awareness challenges in chapters 3, 4, 5 and 6, so let's get you used to the format. I want you to keep a mental note of those unhelpful thought types and start to notice when your Inner Caveman is out and about. When you become aware of the unhelpful thought, I want you to record:

- What was the situation?
- What was the unhelpful thought?
- What type of thought is it?

You can use a notebook or the notes app in your phone to capture some quick reflections; if you want to go a bit deeper, feel free to explore the scenario in your journal. You don't have to record it straight away, but try to be mindful of the awareness challenge and jot down the situations and thoughts as soon as you can.

To help you with this challenge I have created the following examples to demonstrate how you may record situations and your corresponding unhelpful thought and type.

Example 1:

What was the situation?

- I was at work, and my line manager asked me to a meeting at 1pm but didn't say what it was about. I began to feel anxious, and my brain started whirling about what he might want to talk to me about. I convinced myself I was being made redundant.

What was the unhelpful thought and type?

- Thought: I'm going to be made redundant
- Type: Catastrophising

Example 2:

What was the situation?

- Mum assumed I'd be going to her house for Christmas this year. It's our daughter's first Christmas, and we want to spend it just the three of us, but I feel like I should go to Mum's, and I will feel guilty if I don't.

What was the unhelpful thought and type?

- Thought: I should go to Mum's
- Type: Shoulds

Example 3:

What was the situation?

- I felt terrified. My brother lives on his own and has asthma, so what if he catches coronavirus, what if he can't breathe, what if he can't call an ambulance, what if he needs me and I'm not there?

What was the unhelpful thought and type?
- Thought: What if my brother ...?
- Type: What if ...?

As you read through these examples, did you notice how the unhelpful thought created a strong feeling? In example 1 the catastrophising led to fear and then anxiety. In example 2 the should thought created guilt. Finally, in example 3 the "What if ...?" game brought on fear to the point of terror. Our Inner Caveman is responsible for creating many unnecessary feelings, and this is why we will be moving on to look at feelings in the next chapter. For now, continue with the challenge and start to pay attention to your thoughts.

Key aha! moments

Phew, you have made your way to the end of chapter 2. What an adventure! It was packed full to the rafters of useful information and insights, so let's recap on those key learnings:

1. Some people refer to their Inner Caveman as an inner negative voice, their Inner Critic, overthinking or over-worrying.
2. It's normal to have an inner negative voice; it's our survival brain's way of keeping us safe. While it may keep us safe in life-threatening situations, the cost of letting our Inner Caveman run wild is overthinking, overwhelm, anxiety and self-doubt.

3. Don't buy into the myth of your Inner Caveman keeping you motivated and being a high achiever; you can't beat yourself into doing something without beating yourself up in the process.

4. Spotting our Inner Caveman is the key to stopping it creating havoc. We do this by getting up close and personal with it. We name it, describe it and become aware of its favourite types of unhelpful thoughts. These may include:

- Labelling: I'm an idiot
- Mind reading: They think I'm stupid
- Catastrophising: I've missed the train, so I'm going to lose my job
- Shoulds: I should be perfect
- Phoneyism: I'm an imposter
- Overgeneralising: Everything is terrible
- Comparison: They have a much better life than me
- Discounting the positive: I only got the job as no one else applied
- "What if ...?" thoughts: What if this happens? What if that happens?

CHAPTER 3

Feeling far from fine

"I'm fine."

EVERYBODY

If I had a pound for every time I said "I'm fine" when I wasn't, I would be writing this book in the Maldives rather than in South East London. Like the time my 80-year-old neighbour asked me how I was at 7:30am on a cold winter's morning and I said "Yeah, I'm fine thanks, Jim", rather than "I've been awake since 4am worrying about meeting my line manager, and I feel so anxious I think I might be sick". Then, of course, there was the time I said "I'm fine" to a waiter as I didn't think he'd want to know I was worrying whether I had left the straighteners on and my house was burning down at that very moment. If truth be told, sometimes it's just not the right time, place or person for sharing those inner thoughts and feelings, so the classic "I'm fine, thanks" will do nicely.

Of course, there are many moments when I'm not fine. For example, I have felt sad from reading a news story, fear about a pending GP visit, frustration at the other half putting their plate by the dishwasher and not in the dishwasher again (honestly, how many more times do I have to say it ...), all before 9am.

We can all experience a multitude of feelings in a day and many of them will simply pass in the moment. The problem is, though, sometimes our uncomfortable feelings linger like a bad smell and, unless we find a way to shift them, they can leave us feeling far from fine.

In my twenties, I was the queen of stuffing down feelings but, like an unwanted visitor, those feelings just wouldn't go away. Looking back, it's obvious I was overwhelmed by the many feelings swirling around; however, at the time, I wasn't really sure how to name them, let alone how to let them out safely. Of course, Brian didn't help. His over-worrying and constant negative chatter just added more feelings into the mix. If creating fear and unleashing anxiety was Brian's goal, he was on his A game in my twenties. Then there was the niggling self-doubt that whispered "I'm not good enough" at every opportunity, creating a never-ending flow of shame. Just to make matters worse, I had a habit of people-pleasing, which meant I often felt full of resentment too.

Yep, now it's easy to understand what I was feeling and why, but at the time I had no idea what was going on. I just kept telling myself I was fine. Turns out this is the most common lie people tell us; but it's also the most harmful lie when we tell it to ourselves.

10 tell-tale signs of feeling far from fine

If we can feel a multitude of feelings in any given day, how do we recognise when these feelings are becoming too much?

Here are the 10 tell-tale signs:

1. Frequently feeling a range of emotions from fear, guilt and shame to anger and resentment
2. Often referring to yourself as being overwhelmed
3. Regularly feeling anxious
4. Waning resilience (feeling less able to cope or bounce back)
5. Frequently catching colds or suffering with migraines or familiar aches and pains
6. Difficulty dropping off to sleep or waking up before your alarm
7. Frequently feeling low in mood
8. Comforting, for example with food and drink
9. Avoiding feelings by withdrawing from people, situations or new opportunities
10. Over-planning or constant checking to minimise uncertainty and fear

 Grab your journal and a cuppa and take some time here to reflect on which of these tell-tale signs resonate with you the most. Remember to push the emergency brake if you need to.

Why do we feel far from fine?

As I talked about in chapter 1, sometimes it's natural for us to suffer because of tragic life events, but even during the good times we can still suffer. It will come as no surprise to you that our annoying little Inner Cavemen can be one of the reasons for this. Not only do they create lots of unnecessary feelings with their outdated rules, but they also hold us back from talking about our feelings. Nope, that's far too vulnerable for them, so they would rather we stay in our comfort zone and stuff those feelings down. Very unhelpful. Thanks for nothing, Brian.

We also find ourselves drowning in shame when we chase our worth. Many of us internalise those should messages around us and tell ourselves we will only be worthy when we attain those elusive WoW factors, the never-ending list of things we are told we should be or should do.

I prefer to define these WoW factors as a Web of Worth. Just like flies in a spider's web, we become trapped by those should messages woven around us. Instead of owning our inherent worth we find ourselves stuck in shame. Urgh, shame really is one of the most painful and crippling feelings. In counselling training we are taught that all feelings are healthy and to welcome them all in; but, if I'm really honest, I'm more inclined to hide under the duvet till shame goes away. Unfortunately, when shame is left to fester, it becomes the most dangerous of all feelings because it erodes our sense of self.

It's not just following our WoW factors that leads us to feel far from fine. The should messages within our society and cultures also dictate who should and shouldn't feel certain emotions. White men are deemed weak if they show any feeling apart from anger, whereas black women are vilified if they show any anger. These strong messages lead people of all races, ethnicities, genders and cultures to hide, deny or stuff down feelings, leading to significant consequences.

The final, and arguably the most important, reason why we suffer even in the good times is down to how we were taught to recognise and express our feelings as children. If our parents paid attention to our emotional needs by asking us how we felt and giving us a space to talk about feelings safely then that's blooming fantastic. If they modelled talking about their own feelings openly and safely, even better. The thing is, though, this is pretty rare, as us humans haven't quite got the knack of this yet. Sure, better education is out there about the importance of feelings and mental health in general, but people still really struggle with this and tend to pass it on to their kids.

Unfortunately, as we are about to learn, even though the people who brought us up were doing their best, this lack of awareness leads to a huge cost for many of us.

The cost of avoiding our feelings

While feelings were not really talked about in our house in 1980s Britain, there were plenty around, and I was drowning in them. With hindsight, it wasn't my parents' fault; they had been handed down a guide to parenting from their parents, which in turn had been handed down to them by their Victorian parents. The guide pretty much read: provide a roof over your family's head, feed them, educate them and make sure everything they do impresses the neighbours. I mean it's not a bad plan, as such; it provided basic safety and covered most of my physical needs, but it meant my parents had little understanding of their own emotional and mental health needs, let alone mine.

My Dad carried a lot of anger, and when it came out, it was terrifying. I lost count of the times I would see him rage at little things, like my Mum's slightly overcooked dinner. When it was my turn to be the butt of his anger, it was mainly because I didn't live up to who he thought I should be or how I should be performing. My Mum also had a huge amount of feelings bubbling underneath the surface, but she stuffed them deep, deep down. There was no room for feelings in our house; my parents had no idea how to express feelings in a healthy way, so neither did I.

It would take me years to realise that my Dad's feelings were like an iceberg; the anger on the surface but underneath a huge festering lump of other feelings.

While anger can be a healthy feeling, it is often the only culturally acceptable feeling to display, especially for white men. Unfortunately, if you don't deal with all the feelings under the surface, anger will jump out of you like the unexpected Jack-in-the-box. Scroll through your Twitter feed or any other social media platform and you will see people exploding over each other. Carrying unexpressed feelings is painful, and sometimes people in pain lash out at others. My Dad didn't mean to scare me, upset me or invoke shame but this is how I felt, and I didn't know what to do with those feelings apart from cry myself to sleep at night and then stuff them down when I went to school. I carried these feelings around with me for years; the shame eroded my self-worth, the fear held me back and my sadness weighed me down.

Through not recognising these feelings, or having a safe place to express them, I, like many others, found unhelpful coping mechanisms to numb them. I was not a feel the fear and do it anyway kind of person, I was more a feel the fear and numb it with either chocolate or beer kind of person. I needed a beer or glass of wine in hand at all social gatherings (it was either that or avoid going) and chocolate on standby in the cupboard for anything that would take me out of my comfort zone. It never got to the level of drinking on the way to work, but it was enough to affect my sleep and my performance the next day. It also created a great opportunity for my Inner Caveman, Brian, to kick off with "I'm an idiot. Why did I drink all that wine last night?" This, in turn, created a wave of shame. When we numb feelings with booze, food, drugs or something else we start a vicious circle: instead of escaping our feelings, we just pile on new ones.

Leaving our feelings to fester can lead to many other issues. Some may find themselves with a prolonged low mood, while others can feel like they live in a constant state of overwhelm. Being in either of these states leaves our emotional bucket full to the brim. We can therefore lose our patience quickly or withdraw from situations and people because we can't cope with any more.

When our emotional bucket is full, it also has an impact on our body too because feelings have a physical effect. For example, fear creates anxiety and the hormones released suppress our immune system, leading to frequent colds or ill-health. I'll talk about this further in the next chapter, but there is no doubt that our body pays a handsome price when we avoid our feelings.

The worst cost of all comes from suppressing shame. It's a feeling that kicks the legs out from under us and delivers a sucker punch to our gut. It feels so painful because it corrodes our sense of self. We are essentially left believing we are wrong and have no worth or value. An example of the extreme danger of shame is shown by the numbers of people who die by suicide. In 2018 the Samaritans reported that men were three times more likely to die by suicide than women. While all genders have pressure to be a certain way, men are besieged by shame-inducing messages throughout cultures far and wide. They are told they should be strong and shouldn't talk about their feelings. These "man up" messages cause excruciating levels of shame and I believe their contribution to this trend can't be denied.

The costs of ignoring our feelings are high, not only for us individually but also for us as a society. While it may seem scary now to finally look within and work with your feelings, it is something you, and the generations after you, will be forever grateful for.

How to recognise your feelings

In chapter 9 you are going to learn how to empty your emotional bucket and express those feelings safely. However, before you can do this you first need to be able to recognise two things:

- When you are gripped by a feeling
- When those feelings start to build up and become overwhelming

That all sounds fairly simple, doesn't it? Unfortunately, it's made a little bit trickier as there is no universal list of feelings. This means when I say I'm sad, you may say you're upset; or if I say I'm happy, you may say you feel content. Therefore, you need to be able to recognise your feelings and understand what they mean for *you*. To do this, I'm going to ask you to work through two exercises.

Exercise 1: Feelings check-in

The check-in is a simple practice that allows you some time and space to be curious about your feelings. You can do this by writing in your journal or simply taking 10 minutes out in a quiet space. I want you to reflect on how you have been feeling over the past week. Try to identify your specific feelings and how you knew you were feeling this way. As sharing is caring, as always I'm going to share my check-in with you, and then I'll help you with yours.

Zoe's check-in May 2020

I am currently riding the coronavirus emotional rollercoaster so there are many feelings around this week including:

- **Fear**: The recent UK government update on the coronavirus situation left me feeling fearful. I could tell I was fearful because I could feel the anxiety rushing through my body, my heart was beating faster and my breath became shorter.
- **Low mood**: On Thursday I felt blue, my energy levels were low and everything I did took more time than usual. It was like swimming through treacle. Everything seemed more difficult.
- **Anger**: On my daily walk an overenthusiastic jogger brushed past me in the street and I felt a rush of anger. I felt a surge of energy travel up my chest and into my arms and face. I felt tense, hot and bothered.

- **Relief**: I practised yoga online and felt my muscles relax and the tension leave my body.
- **Relaxed**: After doing a 10-minute meditation, my brain was peaceful, my body was at ease and I felt a sense of calm.
- **Happy**: When catching up with my best friend online with a glass of wine, I was laughing, smiling and joking. My body felt at ease.
- **Joy**: On receiving good news, I was beaming from ear to ear and I felt an increase in my energy levels.

As you can see, this doesn't have to be an epic deep and meaningful; it can just be a simple inventory to see what feelings are around.

Now it's your turn.

- Find a place where you feel comfy and won't be disturbed
- Take a few long, deep breaths just to settle your brain and body
- Now think about your week and try to identify when you were gripped by a feeling
- How would you define those feelings, and what were the signs you were gripped?
- Jot this down in your journal or make mental notes

When working through this exercise, please remember the emergency brake rule: in order to go forward safely, you need to be able to stop. If any exercise becomes too much, take some time out to look after yourself.

Exercise 2: Recognising when you feel overwhelmed

You need to be able to recognise when your emotional bucket becomes dangerously close to overflowing. Think back to a time when you felt overwhelmed. Explore your:

- **Feelings**: Describe how it felt (for example, heavy, out of control, full)
- **Thoughts**: Were they confused, looping, critical, something else?
- **Physical sensations**: How did your body feel? Did you feel those familiar aches and pains? Did you have trouble sleeping perhaps?
- **Behaviour**: How did you cope? Did you numb your feelings? Did you withdraw or avoid them, or pretend it wasn't happening?

Feelings can be tricky little beasts so thanks for bearing with me on these exercises. Hopefully even just by recognising your feelings you will notice they have less power over you. Turns out the more we ignore feelings the harder they cling on, but when we acknowledge them, they are no longer in control.

Awareness challenge

In chapter 9 you are going to learn how to express your feelings safely so you can start to feel fab. Don't worry, this doesn't mean I'm going to encourage you to tell your next-door neighbour how you are really feeling on that cold Wednesday morning, but I am going to help you get those feelings out so you don't have to stuff them down or numb them.

Now you know a little more about your feelings, let's continue to grow your awareness. Just to recap, the awareness challenge is all about getting curious in your daily life. In chapter 2 you started to pay attention to unhelpful thought types, and now you are going to tune into your feelings. When a situation arises that invokes a feeling, I want you to grab your journal or the notes app in your phone and work through the following prompts:

- What was the situation?
- What were the signs you were gripped by a feeling or were feeling overwhelmed?

Again, here are a few made-up examples to show you how to log this information.

Example 1:
What was the situation?
- Argh! I sent an email to the wrong person at work.

What were the signs you were gripped by a feeling?
- I felt gripped by shame. I knew it was shame because my Inner Caveman beat me up for making a mistake and I physically wanted to hide!
- I also felt gripped by fear. My body felt really tense, I felt sick and my heart was beating really fast.

Example 2:

What was the situation?

- I was wide awake on Thursday at 4am. I was thinking about my ex and our breakup, and I felt awful.

What were the signs you were overwhelmed?

- Feelings: I was full of feelings – upset, hurt, anger, resentment. I thought I was going to burst.
- Thoughts: Ruminating over every detail of the relationship.
- Physical sensations: Crying a lot. I was exhausted and didn't leave my bed till the afternoon.
- Behaviour: I drank my way through a bottle of wine but it didn't help.

Remember, awareness is the key to change, so take your time with this challenge. Feel free to put the book down for a few days and tune into those feelings.

Key aha! moments

Annnnnnd that's a wrap on chapter 3. Feelings are indeed tricky beasts, so let's recap on the key takeaways:

1. "I'm fine" is a common cultural response or defence strategy when it's not appropriate (time/place/ person) to open up about our real feelings.
2. It's very typical to have a wide range of feelings through any given day. However, when feelings are painful, intense or linger too long, we can

feel uncomfortable. When we have many of these feelings, our emotional bucket overflows and we feel overwhelmed.

3. There is a huge cost to ignoring our feelings. If we stuff them down they lead to feeling overwhelmed, hurting others, numbing behaviours, avoidance behaviours and disconnection.

4. Being able to check in with ourselves and recognise when we are gripped by a feeling or feeling overwhelmed is the first step to taking back control of our feelings.

CHAPTER 4

Tell-tale signs of an anxious body

Every cell in your body is eavesdropping on your thoughts.

DEEPAK CHOPRA

During my high-flying insurance career, I became a fully paid-up member of the 4am wide-awake club. For some reason, my Inner Caveman decided 4am was the optimal time to ruminate over the previous day's events or worry about, well, everything really. While I was more than willing to leave this analysis until a more sensible hour, these thoughts created what seemed like an irreversible chain reaction. They stirred up uncomfortable feelings, sending adrenaline coursing through my body, leaving me wide-eyed and on full alert. More often than not, after staring at the ceiling for a few hours, I would give up on trying to fall back to sleep and haul myself into the shower. As the water flowed, so did my anxiety; more unhelpful thoughts making my tummy flip over, my breath shorten and my heart beat faster. As I quickly grabbed my clothes and got ready for work, I barely acknowledged anyone or anything as I was so caught up in a whirlwind of anxiety.

Next, I would jump on the train and stand under someone's armpit for 22 long minutes; my body remained tense as a result. Once at work, I always began by opening up my emails; again, I would feel immediately anxious as Brian catastrophised about the contents, sending my body into a frenzy.

As the day unfolded, I'd be put on the spot numerous times, and I found myself riding through meetings on caffeine and adrenaline. I had no time for a tea break, let alone a lunch break, so I would grab a sandwich and eat at my desk. When I knew there was potential for conflict, those butterflies in my stomach turned into a flock of seagulls, and I'd need to go to the loo a few times. I'd then often spend my commute home raking over the day's events; as my thoughts looped, the anxiety would again surge through my body.

Once home I would grab a glass of wine to take the edge off; it dulled my thoughts, numbed my feelings and calmed my body. I'd watch the latest TV drama, my body responding to every twist and turn. I'd go to bed at 10:30pm exhausted and fall straight to sleep; then I'd be awake, I'd look at the clock, it would be 4am, and Brian would start to overanalyse the previous day's events.

Sure, not all days were like this, but it can be the norm rather than the exception for many of us. Some of us can feel anxious from the moment we open our eyes in the morning. For others, it may start when they step into the shower and start worrying about the day ahead. For most, though, anxiety can feel like an unwelcome constant companion throughout the day and impossible to turn off.

 Having explored your anxiety-inducing thoughts and feelings in the previous two chapters, you are now going to delve into understanding your anxious body. Before you move on though, take a moment to think about when you feel anxious. Does my hectic day and my anxious brain and body sound familiar to you?

10 tell-tale signs of an anxious body

Our bodies are wired to have two basic physical states: we can be in either a calm state or an anxious state. Here are 10 tell-tale physical signs of an anxious state:

1. Uncomfortable, fast heartbeat
2. Short, quick breaths into your chest
3. Stomach churning or fluttering, often called butterflies, leading you to need the loo more
4. Tensed muscles
5. Difficulty concentrating and poor memory
6. Sweaty, with heat creeping up your body
7. Nauseous
8. Wobbly legs
9. Dry mouth, difficulty in swallowing
10. Wide, dilated eyes

Why do we go into an anxious state?

In life-threatening situations, our Inner Cavemen truly earn their keep. Without my little fella and my body's reaction, I doubt I would be alive. Take, for instance, that time when I was crossing the road and was too caught up in listening to my music to notice a car approaching.

You know that moment where time slows down, your body feels like you've just downed 10 cups of coffee and your tummy is flipping like an Olympic gymnast? Yep, that happened. This was because the little Caveman in my brain finally got catastrophising right for once and shouted "Get out of the way! You are going to die!" (Or words to that effect, with the possibility of an expletive or two.) On hearing Brian's voice, my body reacted by going into an anxious state, thus releasing various hormones. These helped my heartbeat quicken, moving the blood and oxygen around my body to my main leg and arm muscles so I could run. It then tried to empty my bladder and stomach, so I was lighter to run away, and it pumped hormones to my brain so I could just focus on the danger. It even pumped hormones around me to help my skin heal, should I get injured.

The outcome? In a split second I did a sprint to the pavement that Usain Bolt would have been proud of, and I even had the energy for a little "sorry" wave to the driver. Now, while I'm not a fan of my body trying to empty my bladder mid road, I am super grateful for the surge of anxiety because that could have ended very differently.

You may have heard of this reaction described as the fight or flight response. Our body is basically flooding us with anxiety to help us run away from a threat or fight our way to freedom. This means our:

- Lungs expand to get more oxygen into our blood
- Heart beats faster to pump the blood and oxygen around our body quicker
- Blood vessels constrict to divert the blood and oxygen to the big leg and arm muscles so we can run or fight
- Sweat glands sweep into action to keep us cool
- Pupils dilate so we can see more of the threat
- Gut empties to make us lighter
- Thinking brain is turned off so we can focus on the threat
- Blood increases its ability to clot so we can mend should we get injured

Where our Inner Caveman lets us down is when he perceives something as a threat that just isn't life-threatening. Being squished on a packed commute; giving a presentation; making a mistake; not living up to who we are told we should be. These are all things that may feel uncomfortable but aren't life-threatening. Unfortunately, our Inner Caveman still flags them as a threat, and our body dutifully responds by turning on our anxious state, time and again, throughout the day.

We, of course, can't lay the blame for our anxiety solely on our Inner Caveman. Our modern-day on-the-go lifestyles leave little opportunity for us to switch into a calm state. While the adrenaline and endless cups of coffee may help catapult us through the day, it puts our bodies under a huge amount of pressure. With little time to catch our breath, it is no wonder anxiety is so widespread. According to the Mental Health Foundation, in 2013 there were 8.2 million reported cases of anxiety in the UK, making it the most common mental health disorder along with depression. I think you will agree this is a very worrying statistic indeed.

The cost of being stuck in an anxious state

The physical impact of frequently being anxious is high. The hormones released suppress our immune system, constrict our arteries and play havoc with our stomachs. Our bodies were only meant to do this once or twice a week when we needed to outrun the sabre-toothed tiger, but now our anxious state is switched on and off all day. When this occurs too often, we may experience one or more of the following long-lasting symptoms:

- Familiar aches and pains
- Regular headaches or migraines
- Stomach aches
- Colds and flu
- Panic attacks
- Sleeping difficulties
- Fluctuating appetite
- High blood pressure

Being in an anxious state for most of the day can also lead us down the slippery slope of quick fixes. Have you ever tried to trick your body into a calm state by drinking a glass of wine? If so, you are not alone; in 2018 Drinkaware, based in the UK, assessed 6000 adults and 60% responded to say they drink alcohol to cope with the stresses of daily life. While I am a fan of a nice glass of red, we have to be really aware of why we are drinking. Is it because it's a lovely sunny evening and we just fancy a nice cold beer, or is it because we have had another hectic day and want to take the edge off? Short term we can get away with this, but when it becomes our go-to coping mechanism then we need to be very careful as this could lead us to a whole new set of problems.

In addition, being in an anxious state affects our ability to remember stuff and concentrate. With our bodies primed to focus only on the danger, our thinking brain is often switched off, making connecting with tasks and people in the moment really challenging. Again, we can get away with that a few times, but if we are constantly unable to listen to our other half when we get home from work, for example, then it's going to start to erode the relationship.

Lastly, feeling anxious can feel so uncomfortable that we just start avoiding life. More than just withdrawing from people, this can be full-on avoidance of people and places, and at its very worst it can stop us leaving the house.

How to recognise when you are in an anxious state

One of the most powerful aha! moments for my clients usually comes when they understand the link between their routine and their anxiety. While most of us already know activities like presentations trigger those hormones, it's often the smaller, seemingly innocent activities that really begin to pile on the anxiety throughout the day. For example, checking emails upon waking, flicking through social media, back-to-back meetings, reading the news on the way home and binge-watching crime shows can all lead to being stuck in an anxious state for most of the day. What we are not doing is telling too. Skipping breakfast and lunch breaks and having zero breathing space in a day keeps our brain and body on the go and that anxiety flowing. With this in mind, you are going to do two exercises to help you understand the link between your routine and your body state.

Exercise 1: Your tell-tale signs

Before you can expose those anxiety-inducing activities you need to be aware of the signs of when you are anxious. Some people will feel immediately tense, while others will notice a rapid heartbeat. For me it's a somersaulting tummy, a fast heartbeat and difficulty in concentrating. Here is the tell-tale signs list again. Take a moment to identify how you recognise when your body is anxious:

1. Uncomfortable, fast heartbeat
2. Short, quick breaths into your chest
3. Stomach churning or fluttering, often called butterflies, leading you to need the loo more
4. Tensed muscles
5. Difficulty concentrating and poor memory
6. Sweaty, with heat creeping up your body
7. Nauseous
8. Wobbly legs
9. Dry mouth, difficulty in swallowing
10. Wide, dilated eyes

. . . .

Exercise 2: Anxiety-triggering activities

Now let's use this knowledge to help you identify your most anxiety-inducing activities. This exercise can be completed to different depths. If you just want a taster then choose a typical day this week, log your activities and identify if you felt either anxious or calm. If you want to go a little deeper, you can track your activities over the period of a week. Feel free to go into as much detail as you would like.

As I've become much more aware of my own routine and what I need to keep myself calm these days, here is an example based on my general observations over the past two decades.

Example:
Tamara lives with her partner and has two children. She works as an account manager in Manchester.

Activities: 3am–9am
- Woke up at 6am and checked work emails – Anxious
- Quick shower fretting about the day ahead and went through motions of getting dressed – Anxious
- Quickly got kids up and ready for school – Anxious
- Commuted to work, read newspaper and checked social media – Anxious

Activities: 9am–12pm
- Chatted with Jane about weekend – Calm
- Made coffee – Calm
- Checked work emails – Anxious
- Checked phone, replied to the school mums WhatsApp group, checked news and social media – Anxious
- Wrote report – Calm
- Meeting 1: Giving update – Anxious
- Meeting 2: Team meeting, just listening – Calm
- Client presentation – Anxious

Activities: 12pm–6pm
- 15-minute walk at lunchtime – Calm
- 15 minutes on social media – Anxious
- Headphones on, worked listening to music – Calm
- Called client to give difficult news – Anxious
- Conflict in final meeting of the day – Anxious

Activities: 6pm–12am
- Commute, replaying final meeting in head – Anxious
- Made dinner – Calm
- Put kids to bed – Calm
- Finished report – Anxious

- Watched news – Anxious
- Checked emails before bed – Anxious

Analysis
Even though Tamara hasn't gone into detail about her routine we can still see some telling patterns emerging:

Pre-work:
- Anxiety flows where our focus goes. By checking emails first thing, Tamara's brain started the day worrying and found it difficult to stop because she didn't have any calming activities before work. This meant she could barely remember having a shower because she was so distracted by work and she went through the motions of getting ready without paying attention to herself or those around her.
- To make matters worse she used the commute to read the news and scroll through social media, but this triggered unhelpful negative thoughts, uncomfortable feelings and more anxiety.
- Zero activities before 9am to help her feel calm.

During work:
- Tamara's Inner Caveman was loud during presentations and meetings when put on the spot, thus creating more anxiety.
- Checking notifications, emails and social media also triggered more anxiety, but connecting with colleagues, taking a break and listening to music induced a calm state.

After work:
- By using the commute to ruminate on the day, the anxiety kept flowing. This was exacerbated by working in the evening and rechecking emails.
- When she was connected to the task of cooking and reading the kids a story, she became calm.

Summary:
Of the 23 activities logged by Tamara, only 8 led to a period of calm, meaning 65% led her to feel anxious. In my experience, this is fairly typical and, if Tamara had logged the time spent in each state, I would be willing to bet the proportion of time she spent feeling anxious would have been even higher. In order to bring more calm into her life, there are some small changes she could make straight away, like swapping checking her emails first thing to having 15 minutes to herself in the morning to just be. Or switching her news reading on her commute to listening to a funny podcast.

Now it's your turn. Like I say, if you just want a taster then choose a typical day this week, log your activities and identify if you were in either an anxious or calm state. When you have finished this exercise, take some time to analyse your results.

Based on your analysis, can you identify any small changes that can help you going forward?

Here are some examples:

- ***Reducing anxiety-inducing activities****: Are you doing any activities that you can commit to dropping now? Can you leave your phone in another room when you go to bed so you don't check those emails first thing in the morning? Can you commit to not looking at social media till the evening or leaving the news till later in the day? What can you cut out today?*
- ***Calming activities****: Can you commit to adding in more you time? Remember, it doesn't have to be epic to make a difference. Just 10 minutes in the morning for a cup of tea or being mindful in the shower can help. Alternatively, can you take a full lunch break twice a week or grab a coffee and cake every Friday morning? Identify what would work for you.*

In the second half of this book, you will learn how to take back control of the anxiety in various ways, but for now let's spend a little more time growing your awareness.

Awareness challenge

You know the drill. Let's build on your awareness of how anxiety manifests itself in your day by getting curious. Over the coming days pay attention to your body and answer the following questions:

- What was the situation or activity that led you to feel anxious?
- What were the physical signs you were in an anxious state?

As you can see from the following made-up examples, you don't need to write too much. The mere act of taking time to notice and write the situations down along with the signs will be enough to greatly enhance your awareness.

Example 1:
What was the situation?
- I had to tell one of my team it wasn't okay for them to turn up to work in jeans when they were meeting a client.

What were the physical signs you were in an anxious state?
- My heart was pumping really fast beforehand, and I felt really hot as I was speaking to her. Sensations subsided once it was over.

Example 2:

What was the situation?

- I turned off the alarm this morning and noticed I had some notifications. I then spent 20 minutes looking at emails and texts.

What were the physical signs you were in an anxious state?

- I felt panic, my breathing was short and I felt tense all over my body.

Understanding when anxiety shows up in your life and where you feel it in your body is going to be instrumental in helping you conquer it, and I'll help you do that in chapter 10. Your hard work will soon be rewarded, so hang in there.

Key aha! moments

That's chapter 4 done and dusted. There's lots to learn and digest so, as usual, let's recap:

1. Our bodies are wired to have two physical states, calm or anxious.
2. An anxious state occurs when our brain perceives a threat. Our body then turns on our alarm system, the fight or flight response, flooding us with hormones, which helps us to run away or fight.
3. In real life-threatening situations this is super helpful, but our alarm system hasn't been updated to help

us navigate the modern-day world, so our anxiety can be triggered throughout the day.

4. The tell-tale signs of the fight or flight response include: tight chest, racing heart, shallow breath, flipping stomach, tense muscles.

5. If we are in the anxious state too often, this can lead us to have frequent headaches, colds, aches and pains, and sleep issues.

6. There is a cost to our overall wellbeing when we try to force our bodies into a calm state using drink, drugs, food or another comforter, and at its worst anxiety can lead us to avoid people and places.

7. There is often a link between our busy routine and our levels of anxiety.

8. Understanding our specific body sensations and identifying the activities that trigger an anxious or calm state are the first steps to change.

CHAPTER 5

People-pleasing behaviours

When you say "yes" to others,
make sure you are not saying "no" to yourself.

PAULO COELHO

If you find yourself saying yes when you really need to say no then welcome to the people-pleasing club. Many of us recognise this behaviour and would much rather trade off the consequences of doing whatever we have agreed to do than disappoint someone. I always used to put other people's needs first, and I just couldn't see the harm. Who cares if I said yes and stayed late again to finish another report even though I was still tired from the previous months of staying late? So what if I said yes to an outrageously expensive hen do when I was already in my overdraft?

My people-pleasing behaviours weren't just limited to saying yes. I was a dab hand at putting other people's needs first in all kinds of situations. I was the queen of setting flimsy boundaries, like "I will pay for the dinner, and you can pay me back later", and then of course later never came and I wouldn't ask for the money. Or I would say things like "If Carrie is late to meet me again then I'm not going to wait for her", and there I would be an hour later still waiting for her to rock up. On top of that, my people-pleasing behaviour meant I avoided conflict like the plague, so there was no chance of me telling Carrie I was frustrated by her being late all the time.

I told myself all this people-pleasing wasn't a big deal, but that wasn't the case. Putting others' needs first was having a huge impact on my own needs. It battered not only my finances and relationships but also my mental, emotional and physical needs. It meant I was letting my Inner Caveman run wild, it added more feelings to my already full emotional bucket and it filled my day with yet more anxiety. Despite these obvious consequences, I just couldn't stop, and it wasn't until I started working for a charity that I got the wakeup call I needed.

Here I ended up taking on way too much work and responsibility. I was looking after the needs of my manager, the needs of an underfunded charity and the needs of clients. Over time, not only did the resentment build and fracture relationships, but I also started to slowly break. My Inner Caveman had a field day telling me I should be fine and be able to cope, but I felt overwhelmed, unmotivated and I had migraines. It carried on until one day I woke up and I couldn't put one foot in front of the other to get to work. That, my friends, is the classic route to burnout. Put others' needs first, beat yourself up and voila, burnout. It wasn't my finest hour (pun intended).

While you may not have reached burnout, do you recognise any of these behaviours? Take a moment to think about when you put others' needs first. Are you saying yes to others and no to yourself?

10 tell-tale signs of people-pleasing

If you often put other people's needs before your own, you may recognise many of these feelings and behaviours:

1. Saying yes when you need to say no
2. Avoiding conflict like the plague
3. Avoiding giving feedback or an opinion
4. Difficulty in setting or maintaining boundaries
5. Difficulty in making decisions involving others
6. Being a great listener and empathic but tending to do this too much for others
7. Finding being assertive difficult
8. Putting tasks for others before self-caring
9. Often feeling bad, guilty, resentful, angry or anxious
10. Feeling exhausted from doing too much

Why do we people-please?

There are three main reasons why we people-please. Firstly, yep you've guessed it, our Inner Cavemen want to keep us safe, so maintaining our position in the tribe by people-pleasing is a very effective way of doing this. They're also very keen on avoiding conflict, as this is a risk to survival, so again they steer us away from conflict by people-pleasing. "Sure, Carrie, it's no problem you were two hours late to meet me again. I got to read my book!"

Secondly, we have all been influenced by one of the most prevalent should messages: "You should put others' needs first." We can hear this message during religious gatherings, in schools and within our families and cultures. When we meet this demand, we are classed as selfless heroes, but when we fail to do this we are quickly labelled as selfish. Many people therefore turn this misguided moral into their WoW factor:

- I will be worthy when I always put other people's needs first
- I will be worthy when I am selfless
- I will be worthy when I'm a good person

I completely understand this is a well-meaning message; however, these beliefs lead us to please our way through life. The simple fact is we can't look after other people unless we look after ourselves too.

Thirdly, as we explored in chapter 1, some people are taught an even more damaging message: "Your needs don't matter at all." This seed is often planted in childhood and can result from abuse and neglect. It can also, however, be planted by well-intentioned parenting gone wrong. If the people who brought us up set inappropriate boundaries for us, managed conflict with us passively or aggressively or said yes on our behalf, we can grow up thinking our needs don't matter. If we were taken to the doctor when we had a funny rash but told to stop whining when we were feeling sad then how are we supposed to know that emotional needs matter? How are we supposed to learn to go to the doctor when our mental health is suffering? How are we supposed to learn to say no when we are unable to go out for dinner because we are feeling overwhelmed and need an early night? If our needs aren't met as a child then we can resort to people-pleasing as an adult simply because we believe our needs don't matter.

The cost of people-pleasing

I told myself all this people-pleasing wasn't a big deal. I even told myself it made me a nice person, but the reality was very different. Whether at work or with friends and family, I would please and please and please and, as I did, the resentment in my emotional bucket would build up and up and up. Instead of going for the healthy option of noticing the resentment and doing something assertive about it, I opted for one of these less healthy options:

1.   Notice I felt resentful towards the person I was people-pleasing and then moan to everyone else in the office/friendship group about it.

2. Notice I felt resentful and then just cut the person out of my life. Ouch.
3. Not notice, stuff it down and pretend it was fine till I blew up.

I've got to admit, none of the three options were particularly helpful, and all three affected many of my personal and professional relationships. However, it was the blowing up that was definitely least helpful because nobody was ever prepared for the usually mild-mannered 5ft Zoe (okay 4ft 11 and ¾ Zoe) turning into the Incredible Hulk. So much so that my best friend still reminds me, in the way only best friends can, of *that* time in 1999 when I exploded in an estate agency and silenced the entire office. It was not pretty, people, and it certainly was not helpful. Turns out people-pleasing doesn't make us nice people after all.

The cost of people-pleasing doesn't stop there; the price is high because we neglect our own needs in the process. For example, I love supporting people. Whether they are counselling clients or my partner, I really enjoy spending my time and energy helping them. However, I know if I did this for 12 hours a day, six days a week, I would burn out in a flash. No matter how much we want to help others, we just can't do it unless we help ourselves too. If we don't attend to our physical, mental, emotional and financial needs, we will become drained. If left for too long, that can lead to burnout. However, if we look after our own needs, while being aware of others, we can lead a kinder, more balanced life.

As if all the above wasn't enough, we also have to realise that the way we behave teaches people how to treat us. If we always put others' needs first, we will attract people who will always take from us. However, if we demonstrate our assertive muscles, showing the world we value our needs, then our needs will be valued in return.

How to recognise your people-pleasing behaviours

Whenever my dog, Paddy, hears the fridge door open, he is up on his feet and by the fridge quicker than you can say sausages. The trigger is the sound of the fridge door opening, and his behavioural reaction is to sprint to the fridge, all with the hope of a reward sausage. Humans are exactly the same; okay, so we don't (usually) run to the fridge for sausages, but we do condition ourselves how to react in certain situations.

This means many of us may have conditioned ourselves to people-please. A common example of this is being asked to stay late at work. We may automatically say yes without thinking. The reward is no uncomfortable silence or response, and we keep in the other person's good books. The not-so-great outcome is that we may be tired and have to renege on existing commitments.

Therefore, to bring our people-pleasing under control, we need to be familiar with our triggers and behaviours, and the next exercise will help you identify yours.

Exercise: Top people-pleasing behaviours

The aim of this exercise is to identify your go-to people-pleasing behaviours. To do this, I want you to mull over the events of the past few months and identify your three most prevalent behaviours. As ever, I will go first with some classic old examples:

Zoe's top people-pleasing behaviours

1. In pole position, we have the notorious people-pleasing behaviour: saying yes when we need to say no.

    Examples:
    - Saying yes to meeting my friends when I really needed self-care instead
    - Saying yes to my line manager when I really needed to go home
    - Saying yes to a really expensive hen do

2. In second place comes being a great listener and empathic but tending to do this too much for others.

    Examples:
    - Being there for friends even when I was exhausted
    - Taking on additional work to help the team out even though I was overloaded
    - Doing volunteer work outside of my day job even though I already had a packed schedule and a full head and heart

3. Last, but by no means least, is difficulty in setting and maintaining boundaries.

Examples:

- Let my flatmate get away with not paying for food again
- Waiting for Carrie for an hour when she was late even though I said I wouldn't
- Allowing Tara to talk to me disrespectfully and not sticking up for myself

Your top people-pleasing behaviours

Take some time to explore each of the eight behaviours below and think about how prevalent they are in your day-to-day life. As you reflect, try to write down some examples of when you engaged in these behaviours.

- Saying yes when we need to say no
- Avoiding conflict like the plague
- Avoiding giving feedback or an opinion
- Difficulty in setting or maintaining boundaries
- Difficulty in making decisions involving others
- Being a great listener and empathic but tending to do this too much for others
- Finding being assertive difficult
- Putting tasks for others before self-caring

How did you find the exercise? Was it all too easy to find examples, or did you struggle? You know the drill: grab your journal and take some time to reflect.

Awareness challenge

In chapter 11 you are going to learn how to tame your people-pleasing behaviours and turn them into assertive action. This doesn't mean you can't be kind and do nice things for others; we are just going to ensure you look after yourself too. Once you learn how to be assertive, you can start to confidently say no without being fearful of the reaction or feeling guilty. Before we work on growing your assertive muscles, let's continue to grow your awareness of your people-pleasing behaviours by doing another awareness challenge.

Over the next few days, I want you to bring awareness to your people-pleasing behaviours. When they occur, grab your journal or notes app in your phone and work through the following:

- What was the situation?
- What was the people-pleasing behaviour?
- What was the impact on your mental, emotional and physical health?

Then, after you have gathered some examples, I want you to reflect on the situations and identify any common themes. For example, do your people-pleasing behaviours often occur with the same person/people? Is it always at work or another environment? When a situation frequently leads to people-pleasing behaviours then we can identify our triggers. Being aware of your triggers is really helpful because, as you will find in chapter 11, it will enable you to prepare your response in advance so you can break the conditioning and take that assertive action instead. For now, though, let's focus on gaining more awareness. Here are a few made-up examples to help you.

Example 1:
What was the situation?
- During the first month of the pandemic I was exhausted, but I thought I wasn't doing enough, so I kept saying yes to picking up shopping for various neighbours and friends.

What was the people-pleasing behaviour and what was the impact on your mental, emotional and physical health?
- I said yes when I needed to say no. My Inner Caveman kept labelling me as lazy, so I started to feel resentful and overwhelmed and I became more anxious and exhausted.

Example 2:
What was the situation?
- My Mum started talking about politics and was very disrespectful about my views. She called me a snowflake.

What was the people-pleasing behaviour and what was the impact on your mental, emotional and physical health?
- I avoided the conflict and did not put boundaries in place. Instead I walked away, but now I feel so angry. It's not okay to talk to me like that, and now I keep ruminating on it and waking up early.

Can you identify any triggers?

- Yes. My Mum. I can often assert myself around others but when it comes to my Mum I fall into people-pleasing behaviours. I really want to stop.

Please be aware, much of our people-pleasing behaviours are conditioned into us, so don't beat yourself up for engaging in them. All I'm asking you to do at this stage is observe your triggers and behaviour with curiosity, not judgement. As ever, if this challenge becomes too much then please take some time out.

Key aha! moments

Congratulations, chapter 5 is in the bag. It was packed full of people-pleasing insights, so let's look back on what you learned:

1. People-pleasing is when we constantly put other people's needs before our own.
2. It's normal to have an inner people-pleaser; it's our survival brain's way of keeping us safe by being part of the tribe.
3. Many of us learned our needs don't matter or it's selfish to put our needs first. However, the truth is we can't look after others unless we look after ourselves too.
4. The cost of letting our inner people-pleaser loose without adequate supervision is resentment, a never-ending to-do list, strained relationships, a

full emotional bucket and physical issues such as exhaustion and burnout.

5. We teach people how to treat us. If we people-please we often attract people who only take from us.

6. Our inner people-pleasers may differ to some extent, but they all have some unhelpful behaviours in common. The first step to changing these behaviours is becoming aware of your most prevalent types and identifying situations (triggers) when they occur.

CHAPTER 6

Pesky self-doubt

Never let self-doubt hold you captive.

ROY T. BENNETT

When I was the grand old age of 8, my English teacher, Miss Jones, who was in fact Welsh (honestly, I'm not making this up), announced to my parents that I needed extra English lessons. Apparently, my ability, or lack of ability, to spell umbrella and put commas in the right places was a major cause for concern. Being teachers themselves, my parents put a huge amount of value on doing well at school, so this news went down like a lead balloon. As a result, I was made to participate in extra lessons at home, and at school. The message was clear: I should be better. And that was all it took to sow the seeds of my self-doubt.

At the age of 9, I sat a series of tests to determine which sets I would be in going forward at school. I can vividly remember sitting at my desk before my Maths test thinking I had to do well to impress my parents. Unfortunately, these thoughts created a surge of anxiety and I just couldn't concentrate on the test. As a result, I was placed in the third set for Maths. I was devastated. I had never liked English, but I thought Maths was my thing and this clearly showed I wasn't good enough at that either. My Dad was angry; again, the message was clear that I should be better. Then something interesting happened. I started to work super hard in Maths to improve my grades and, amazingly, two years later I had reached the top set. I was so pleased; I had worked hard and achieved, and it was an important lesson to learn.

However, the joy was short-lived because those seeds of self-doubt couldn't be unsown. I still didn't believe I was good enough because, by this point, my Inner Caveman had internalised those should messages, always telling me I should be better, I should be achieving more.

Over the course of my school life, those seeds of self-doubt were fed and watered every time I didn't receive top grades, spell a word correctly or hit the right note in music. By the time I was 16, many more seeds of self-doubt had been planted and were growing rapidly. I wasn't like the girls in magazines or other girls in the class; I should have been thin, feminine and taller but when I looked in the mirror all I saw was a small, podgy tomboy. My Dad told me I should apply make-up to cover my freckles and wear heels to make me taller, but I knew it just wasn't me. I wasn't who I should be, and I wasn't doing what everyone told me I should do. Unfortunately, I had grown beliefs about my appearance, personality and sexuality that were far from complimentary and that led me to the most harmful self-doubt belief of all: I'm just not good enough.

Beliefs like "I'm not good enough" or "I'm a failure" are dangerous weeds that spread rapidly through our thoughts, feelings and body. In the counselling world, we refer to them as limiting beliefs as they influence our behaviours and starve us of what we need to grow. Self-doubt, therefore, is more than our Inner Caveman doubting our ability to pull off that presentation or three-point turn. Self-doubt is doubting our very being; it's the painful whispers of not good enough; it's the inability to see who we truly are. It's the never-ending seeking of approval and worth. It's believing we are wrong and drowning in shame as a result.

10 tell-tale signs of pesky self-doubt

If your seeds of self-doubt have bloomed into fully-fledged beliefs about yourself then you may well recognise the following tell-tale signs:

1. Holding limiting beliefs: Often summing up your entire self with a phrase such as "I'm not good enough", "I'm worthless" or "I'm a bad person"
2. Having a skewed sense of self: Finding it difficult to describe yourself, although you can easily point out some negatives
3. Seeking and depending on validation from others
4. Difficulty in accepting positive feedback such as compliments and appraisal points

5. Accepting negative feedback from others without questioning if it's actually true
6. Frequently feeling ashamed and anxious
7. Trying to fit in or hiding parts of yourself
8. Perfecting and procrastinating
9. Stuck in a never-ending cycle of proving your worth, such as "I will be worthy when I ..."
10. Accepting low standards and unhealthy behaviours from others

Why do we doubt ourselves?

Some refer to our childhood years as the best years of our life, but for most of us this is a tricky passage, to say the least. The child development gurus have this period down as the time when we develop our identity, meaning it's the time we realise we are more than an extension of our parents, and we start to form our true self and our understanding of our worth.

As we spend most of our time as children primarily in the home or education system, these environments have a massive impact on how we see ourselves. If our parents provide us with unconditional love, we learn to love ourselves and feel worthy; however, if we start to receive messages about who we should be and what we should be doing then those seeds of self-doubt start to flourish. If we don't receive unconditional love at home, we look to our education system to help us recognise our talents and grow into our true self. Unfortunately, our school systems are under such pressure to perform that, in turn, the pressure is passed on to the students. I've sat across from enough young people in the counselling room to know this leaves many of them believing their worth is dependent on their academic intellect, and ultimately their results.

Outside the home and education system, some children look to social media or celebrities for guidance. Sadly, as we learned in chapter 1, we are all brought up in a world that ranks our worth by various aspects of our identity, such as our race, ethnicity, nationality, gender, sexuality, age, appearance, weight, class, religion or intelligence, so we quickly learn to see parts of ourselves as worthy and lovable while disowning other parts. When teenagers, we then become caught up in chasing the elusive WoW factors – the things we think are going to deliver our worth but, no matter how hard we try, always leave us sorely disappointed.

It doesn't get better as adults; many cultures equate worth with owning a house, driving a nice car or earning a fat salary. We see people get sucked in by messages about money and success, working long hours, usually at the expense of their mental, physical, emotional and connection needs. Are they successful? Some may say yes, but are they fulfilled? Could they feel worthy without the external validation they get from material items?

Culture also dictates that men should be strong and shouldn't show their feelings and women should be perfect, but is that healthy for any of us? The list of conditions of worth goes on and on, so is it any wonder those seeds of self-doubt sown in our childhood become weeds in our adulthood?

Of course, our pessimistic friend in our head, the Inner Caveman, doesn't help us with any of this. Fitting in is the name of his survival game, and if that means denying parts of our true self and pretending we are someone different then so be it. He will tear you down if you try to stand out and he will fill you full of unhelpful negative thoughts to hold you back. Unfortunately, this can leave us caught in a vicious cycle. When we don't think we are good enough, we beat ourselves up, feel shame and hold ourselves back so we can't reach our full potential. We then use this as further evidence that we are not good enough and it strengthens that belief.

The cost of buying into self-doubt

Turns out the limiting beliefs we form from those seeds of self-doubt have immense power. All it took was the inability to spell umbrella, being in the third set for Maths and being chucked out of choir at the age of 10 and I created a limiting belief about my creativity. Disowning that part of myself for decades meant I held myself back from doing anything creative. It wasn't until I worked with a business coach, in my thirties, that I started to question the belief. As soon as my coach suggested blogging about my counselling work, my brain instantly dismissed it.

Of course I couldn't do that as I'm terrible at spelling. As my coach persisted with the idea, she gave me two gifts that were enough to make me question my belief. Firstly, she provided some in-depth training on how to write a blog, reminding me how humans can always learn. Secondly, she believed in me. She gave me the courage to try, and to my amazement I eventually published my first blog. The simple fact is, if she hadn't challenged my limiting belief, I wouldn't be writing this book now.

The cost of holding this belief for 30-odd years though was nothing in comparison to my ultimate self-doubt belief that I'm not good enough. Not only did this belief provide unlimited ammunition to my Inner Caveman, who fell head first into the imposter syndrome trap, but it also left me feeling fearful, anxious and ashamed. For me, shame was like carrying around a bag of lead; it was heavy, painful and exhausting.

To minimise the anxiety and shame, I adapted my behaviour and became a chameleon. I held myself back, stayed small and wore a mask to fit in. However, this behaviour did nothing to build my worth or credibility with myself and instead kept me in a cycle of self-doubt.

When I was visible, I tried to control what people thought of me by being a perfectionist. At the time, I told myself I was just being diligent and that I had high standards; but, make no mistake, I was perfecting due to self-doubt. I would triple-check work, spending needless hours on small tasks, and would leave no *i* undotted or *t* uncrossed. Then if I couldn't make things perfect, I would procrastinate and put things off; after all, you can't be judged if you don't put anything out there.

To make matters worse, as I couldn't validate myself, I sought reassurance from others. I looked to colleagues, friends, family, random people on the internet to provide validation. I absorbed their judgement and feedback like a sponge, never daring to question it. I accepted poor behaviour from others, and I got stuck in unhealthy relationships as a result.

The cost of buying into self-doubt wasn't just limiting beliefs, uncomfortable feelings, unhelpful behaviours and no sense of self-worth; it was also the negative impact it had on my sense of self. I had lost who I was in the race to chase my worth. I lost who I was by playing to the shoulds. I lost who I could have been by holding myself back. I was confused about my true self, and I didn't know how to be me.

How to recognise signs of self-doubt

Oh, pesky self-doubt, how I hate thee. It creates a huge amount of pain and is a complex beast to slay. I decided to leave it till last for you to explore so you could draw on your learnings from previous chapters to help weed out the sneaky little so and so. As ever, the first step to fighting self-doubt is becoming aware of how it rears its head in your life.

There are four ways self-doubt makes itself known:

1. **Limiting beliefs**: When your Inner Caveman bellows out phrases like "Not good enough" or "Bad person" it's a sure indicator your self-doubt is at play.
2. **Feelings**: Bucketloads of shame. This isn't the flash of embarrassment that comes when you trip up on the pavement or the feeling of guilt when you have done something wrong. Shame is the painful feeling that screams you are wrong, leaving you wanting to hide from everyone, including yourself. When your self-doubt rises, so does the shame in your emotional bucket.
3. **Body sensations**: As you learned in chapter 3, shame is a feeling that kicks the legs out from under you and delivers a sucker punch to your gut. By being aware of how your body reacts to shame, you can use this response like an early warning system.
4. **Behaviours**: Your actions can also provide clues to when you are caught in self-doubt. In particular you need to be curious if you are:
    - Holding yourself back from opportunities
    - Being inauthentic or trying too hard to fit in
    - Perfecting and procrastinating
    - Seeking external validation too much

Exercise: Spotting self-doubt

The aim of this exercise is to help you understand when your pesky self-doubt is worming its way into your life. As ever, let's explore mine and then we can explore yours.

Zoe's self-doubt list

- Limiting beliefs: When I didn't get an A grade or when I saw the front cover of a popular magazine with a thin woman featured, my Inner Caveman would bellow "I'm not good enough". This was my go-to phrase about myself.
- Feelings: Shame. Yuk. I know I'm doubting myself when I feel like I am wrong. Not like "Oh, I've just copied down a wrong number" kind of wrong but more like "Argh, I am wrong to my very core!" kind of wrong. Ouch.
- Body sensations: Shame feels like someone has kicked the legs from underneath me. I feel winded and my breath shortens.
- Behaviours:
  - Holding myself back from opportunities
  - Being inauthentic and trying too hard to fit in
  - Perfecting and procrastinating
  - Seeking external validation too much

Tick, tick, tick and a big fat tick. I've done all four. I've held myself back from asking for a pay rise and going for jobs because I just didn't believe I was good enough. I've tried to fit in and pretend I love stuff even though I've hated it. I've perfected to please countless times, going over and above the call of duty, not out of the goodness of my heart but out of a need to control what people thought of me, as I didn't want them to see what I saw. I've also procrastinated and not done things, just so I couldn't be judged.

As for validation, I would seek a lot. My Inner Caveman would dismiss the positive and focus on the negative. For example, when I started writing blogs, I had trouble believing the positive feedback. So I wrote another, and again the feedback was really positive. I still didn't believe it though, so I wrote a few more, and again great feedback. This made me wonder who was right about my creativity. Was it my English teacher or the people who read the blogs? By asking that question, I realised I had fallen into the validation trap. I was seeking validation externally rather than seeking it from within. By getting caught in this trap, I was devaluing myself, eroding my ability to trust myself, and it left me at the mercy of other people's opinions. Not just the opinions of my nearest and dearest, I may add, but the opinions of people I had never even met.

Now it's your turn. When you are ready, start by taking a moment to reflect back on the past few months and then read through the prompts to see if you can spot how your self-doubt usually shows up. Remember, if at any point this exercise becomes overwhelming then please apply your emergency brake.

Your self-doubt list

- Can you identify your limiting beliefs (those negative phrases that pop up on repeat)?
- How do you feel when you doubt yourself?
- Describe the corresponding sensations in your body
- Reflect on the following behaviours and explore how these show up when you start doubting yourself:
    - Holding yourself back from opportunities
    - Being inauthentic and trying too hard to fit in
    - Perfecting and procrastinating
    - Seeking external validation

Awareness challenge

In chapter 12 you are going to learn how to turn your pesky self-doubt into the much healthier self-clout. Note, this does not mean we will pretend you are the most amazing person in the world, nor the worst person in the world. Nope, this is all about being realistic and getting to know who you really are. Before you can start work on growing your self-clout muscles, you first need to learn a bit more about your self-doubt by practising recognising the signs of it kicking off.

This is the last time you'll be doing the awareness challenge in this section of the book, but it won't be the last time you draw on this learning. You know what to do. Look out for events that happen over the coming days where you notice your self-doubt creeping in and answer the following questions:

- What was the situation?
- What were the signs of self-doubt?
  - Limiting beliefs
  - Feeling shame
  - Body sensations
  - Behaviours:
    - Holding yourself back from opportunities
    - Being inauthentic and trying too hard to fit in
    - Perfecting and procrastinating
    - Seeking external validation

Again, here are some examples I have created to help you with your final challenge.

Example 1:
What was the situation?
- The nursery school owner remarked I had been late twice this week to pick up Lucy.

What were the signs of self-doubt?
- Limiting belief: I immediately thought "I'm not good enough".
- Feelings: I felt shame and wanted the ground to swallow me up.
- Body sensations: It felt like my legs had been kicked out from underneath me.
- Behaviours: I sought validation from my partner.

Example 2:

What was the situation?

- I've been in my job for three years and feel the need to change and grow. A role in another team has come up for the grade above, and I have 75% of the skills and experience, but each time I come to do the application form, I just fill up with self-doubt and can't seem to finish it.

What were the signs of self-doubt?

- Limiting belief: "I'm a failure".
- Feelings: I noticed many feelings when filling out the form; I'm fearful, upset and also full of shame.
- Body sensations: Quick heartbeat; felt nauseous.
- Behaviours: I can see I'm holding myself back despite being encouraged by others to apply. This is a pattern I've been repeating for many years.

Example 3:

What was the situation?

- My friend from my singing group said I had obviously enjoyed Christmas and was a little rounder than when she saw me a few months ago.

What were the signs of self-doubt?

- Limiting belief: The comment kept looping round my head, and I started to think I was ugly and fat. I just couldn't beat the judgement away, and I went on to repeat "I'm useless".

- Feelings: At first, I was really angry with her for being so rude, but when I got home I also felt upset and full of shame.
- Body sensations: I felt really hot and bothered.
- Behaviours: I just could not validate myself.

 Before we continue, I just wanted to check in and see how you are feeling after this exercise? It's far from easy exploring your self-doubt, so well done for having the courage to do that. If it has brought up any uncomfortable feelings like shame then please take some time to look after yourself before you continue.

Key aha! moments

Can we have a fanfare, please? Yes, it's time to celebrate. You have grown your awareness and from here on in you are on the up and up. Before we move on, let's have a little recap of this particularly eventful chapter:

1. Self-doubt is more than doubting our ability to do something in the moment; it's repeatedly doubting ourselves to a point where we form limiting beliefs about ourselves.
2. The seeds of self-doubt are sown in our childhood at the same time as our identity is forming.
3. Humans are inherently worthy; however, we have created a world that ranks our worth by various

aspects of our identity. As children, we quickly learn to see parts of ourselves as worthy and lovable while disowning other parts.

4. When we get caught chasing our worth, trying to be the person we think we should be, we lose sight of who we truly are.

5. The cost of self-doubt:

    - We form limiting beliefs about ourselves like "I'm not good enough". These limiting beliefs influence our behaviours and starve us of what we need to grow.
    - We hold ourselves back from opportunities, perfect and procrastinate, and seek validation externally rather than within ourselves.
    - We accept unhealthy behaviour from others, leading to unhealthy relationships.
    - Shame fills our emotional bucket to the brim.

6. Being aware of how our self-doubt shows up in our daily life is the first step towards gaining self-clout.

CHAPTER 7

The messy middle

We delight in the beauty of the butterfly, but rarely admit the changes it has gone through to achieve that beauty.

MAYA ANGELOU

I must admit, there was more than one occasion when I sat opposite my ever-patient counsellor and announced that I wanted to ditch this new-found awareness and go back to living in blissful ignorance. I mean, sure, it was helpful to understand Brian and my people-pleasing behaviours, but this new awareness was accompanied by a slap in the face. I began to regret letting Brian rule my life, I was upset by how much I had lost through feeling anxious and I felt ashamed of my people-pleasing and self-doubting ways. Truth was, though, there was no going back even if I wanted to, because ignorance is never really blissful. With the benefit of hindsight, I can now see I was caught in the messy middle. This is the part of personal growth where we can't go back and unlearn stuff about ourselves but we haven't quite got to the bit where we feel that cathartic change kick in.

If you are feeling overwhelmed by your new-found awareness then let me put your mind at ease; this is normal. Think of this as the part of the process where the caterpillar goes into its cocoon and becomes a gooey mess before regenerating as a beautiful butterfly.

The good news is that, by reading the first six chapters, you are well into your transformation. Each chapter has helped you take steps forward in becoming more aware of your beliefs, thoughts, feelings, body sensations and behaviours. The even better news is, now you are more aware, you can move on to growing your wings. Over chapters 8 to 12 you will learn how to:

- Hush your noisy Inner Caveman and say hello to your healthier Inner Coach
- Express your feelings safely
- Relieve your anxiety and live in a calmer state
- Balance your needs and take assertive action
- Ditch the self-doubt and build your self-clout

 However, before we move on, let's celebrate your hard work. Gaining awareness is by no means an easy feat, but you have invested a huge amount of time and energy in your self-development, and that, my friend, has taken courage. Please take some time to reflect on this and reward yourself with something that makes you smile.

What are your expectations?

The next six chapters are dedicated to taking back control of your health and happiness. I will equip you with techniques and practices that will help you respond to whatever life throws at you.

Before we set off, I want to just double-check you don't have any unrealistic expectations lurking around. For me, there came a point when my awareness had grown, I was using the techniques you are about to learn and I had made huge changes. I was feeling fab, my brain was rational, my body was calm and I thought I was fixed. However, I then noticed I had started people-pleasing again. I was really annoyed with myself. I mean, how many times was I going to do this? I had become aware of the pattern of behaviour, I had learned how to stop it and was saying no a lot more, so how come I had fallen back?

As I talked it through with my counsellor, I asked her the mother of all questions: "When will I be fixed?" She paused and gently delivered the news I clearly didn't want to hear. It wasn't about being broken or fixed; life was, and always is, a never-ending journey of growth.

Reader, I'm not going to lie, I was not satisfied with this answer; I wanted a date and time. I had worked my little socks off understanding myself and wanted to get off this emotional rollercoaster and reap my rewards. She didn't budge, though, and as I pondered this over the following days it slowly dawned on me. I wasn't a broken plate that needed to be glued back together by Christmas. I was human. An ever-growing, fallible human. Ever-growing meaning I could learn, change and take five steps down the path towards living a healthier life, but fallible as in some days I might take a few steps back.

With this realisation came relief; I wasn't aiming to be perfect or fixed. Each day I was striving to be a healthier version of myself so I could move further down the path. I realised no matter how slow my progress, I could never go back to square one.

I have sat across from many clients who too ask me when they will be fixed and I can see the relief when it dawns on them this isn't about being perfect or fixed. I therefore urge you to shift your expectations. Aim to be a healthier version of yourself each day, grant yourself permission to try, and fail, but never give up.

Shifting my expectations was a game-changer in my own journey. I didn't beat myself up when I fell back into old unhealthy ways. Instead I learned from those mistakes and took more steps forward the next day. As I look back on my own journey, and those of my clients, I can see how far we have come using the techniques and practices you are about to learn. Having the right expectations from the outset ensured we never gave up.

The journey to your healthier self is as easy as ABC

So now we need to cover the not-so-tiny matter of how you are going to make the changes you desire, and this is where the ABC technique comes in. "What is that?" I hear you cry. Well, I'm glad you asked.

The ABC technique is three simple steps that will give you all the insight and practices you need to live a healthier and happier life. During the next five chapters, we will go through the technique in more detail with lots of lovely examples, but for now let's explore the steps of the journey.

A is for Awareness

Being aware is the first step to change. It allows us to spot the signs of when we are far from fine. It shines a light on those unhelpful thoughts, uncomfortable feelings, anxious body sensations, pesky beliefs and unhelpful behaviours. It alerts us and helps us make a different choice. When you spot any of the tell-tale signs we explored in chapters 2 to 6, you need to move on to step B.

B is for Brake

This step is vital as it helps us respond to a situation in a healthy way, rather than react in our old unhealthy ways. We tend to react to situations because our brain and body are gripped by uncomfortable feelings and physical sensations, which makes it more difficult for us to think rationally. When we are in the midst of this, we just want to grab something, anything, which takes away the discomfort. This step quickly helps us calm our brain and body, reducing the discomfort and helping us access our more rational thinking brain, our Inner Coach.

In the introduction you learned two ways to apply your emergency brake. As you work through the next five chapters I will introduce you to many more.

C is for Coach

If I listened to Brian morning, noon and night you can bet your bottom dollar I would be overwhelmed, anxious and riddled with self-doubt. The biggest factor that determines our health and happiness is how we talk to ourselves, and coach ourselves, through our daily life. If we learn to talk to ourselves in a way that motivates us to grow and push forward, without beating ourselves up in the process, we venture further down the path to living a healthier and happier life. However, if we listen to our Inner Caveman we will be far from fine.

In the next chapter I will help you to create your own Inner Coach. Then you will equip your Inner Coach with a set of practices that will help retrain your brain, body and behavioural responses. I've used the word practices here because repetition is the key to undoing old unhealthy patterns and creating new ones.

Now, this is not going to click overnight. I had been people-pleasing from an early age so, after 30 years of it, I had conditioned myself to say yes. However, the ABC technique helped me to gain awareness and remain calm so that I could recognise my behaviour and change my response. Each day I tried, and sometimes it didn't quite go to plan, but I carried on learning and developing and, over time, I changed.

Over the next five chapters your Inner Coach will learn:

- Chapter 8: How to think like a coach
- Chapter 9: How to express your feelings safely
- Chapter 10: How to relieve anxiety and be calm
- Chapter 11: How to manage your needs and take assertive action
- Chapter 12: How to know yourself, accept yourself and be yourself in an often judgemental world without getting knocked down and drowning in shame

To use the ABC technique, you are going to need a dose of courage. I wonder what that word brings up for you? For me, courage is the ability to sit with the discomfort of my fear, while trusting myself to deal with whatever happens next. If you know in your heart that there is a deeper purpose for the way your life can unfold, I encourage you to embrace these chapters and be all in with your courage. By reaching into your fear and uncertainty, you can wake up, become aware and embrace being truly alive. Imagine that.

I'll leave the final words in this chapter to an inspirational leader who knew a thing or two about courage.

I learned that courage was not the absence of fear, but the triumph over it. The brave man is not he who does not feel afraid, but he who conquers that fear.

NELSON MANDELA

Key aha! moments

Congratulations, you have already invested a lot of time and energy into your personal development journey. The preceding chapters have helped you grow bucketloads of awareness, and this is going to come in very handy in the following chapters.

Before we move on though, let's recap on chapter 7:

1. The messy middle is the part of personal growth where we can't go back and unlearn stuff about ourselves but we haven't quite got to the bit where we feel that cathartic change kick in.
2. Growing our awareness can be painful at times but being stuck with anxiety, feeling overwhelmed and overthinking is far worse.
3. We are not broken; we don't need to be fixed. We are striving towards living a healthier and happier life by being a healthier version of ourselves each day, not a perfect version.

4. No matter the setbacks or how slow our progress, we never go back to square one.

5. The biggest factor that ultimately determines our health and happiness is how we talk to ourselves, and coach ourselves, through our daily life. In order to do this, we use the ABC technique:

   - **A** is for Awareness: Being aware is always the first step to change
   - **B** is for Brake: Calming our brain and body so we can respond, rather than react, to a situation
   - **C** is for Coach: Learning how to talk to ourselves and help ourselves no matter what life throws at us

CHAPTER 8

Your healthy Inner Coach

Talk to yourself like you would talk to a friend.

COMMON SAYING

I don't know about you but there is no way I would speak to a friend the way I speak to myself. Experts reckon we have about 2000-plus thoughts an hour, so that's a whole lot of random thoughts my friends don't need to hear, ranging from what I want for dinner to trying to guess what my dog is thinking (seriously, does he think about anything other than sausages, squirrels and walkies?). Then there are the bigger meandering thoughts I have about the meaning of life, how to create world peace and whether the Spice Girls were the best girl band ever. (That was a joke; of course they were.) Sure, each of those topics has a time and a place to be said out loud, which is usually after a few beverages, but again I'm not necessarily sure my friends need to hear this.

We know what this common saying is getting at really: we need to be kind and compassionate to ourselves, just like we are to our friends. But what does that really mean? Of course I'm kind to my friends. If I went around calling them an idiot, they wouldn't stay friends for long. But don't we all sometimes take that kindness a bit too far? Haven't we all had a friend who says they feel guilty about not going to the gym and we respond with "No, don't feel guilty. I haven't been for three weeks. Let's order pizza"? They don't want to hear our motivational speech on self-care and of the many benefits of exercise; they want us to let them off the hook and be their pizza buddy.

Then there are the times we blatantly lie to our friends. Like when they ask if you like their new boyfriend, Tim, whom you can't stand, and you say "Yeah, I love Tim. He seems really nice!" And let's not get started on the "Does my bum look big in this?" question; surely we all know the answer to this is *always* no?

It seems being kind doesn't always bring honesty, which raises the question, if our Inner Caveman is too harsh and being friendly is too soft, how do we effectively talk to ourselves? This is where our Inner Coach comes in. This is the part of our brain that isn't run by our survival instincts (aka our Inner Caveman); it is the more rational and, dare I say it, wiser part of our brain. It's the voice that we hear on the fifth day of our holiday when we are fully relaxed, and it says "Why was I so stressed about that email last week? It really doesn't matter in the grand scheme of things", or when we reflect on that problem we had a year ago, which seems so insignificant now. Our Inner Coach is kind and compassionate when it needs to be but also encouraging when we could do more. It's firm but fair, it acknowledges and celebrates our achievements, and it learns from failure and mistakes. It doesn't let us off the hook; it takes accountability for our growth without beating us up in the process.

Ultimately how we talk to ourselves and coach ourselves though the good times in our life, and the downright terrible times, will have a huge impact on our mental, emotional and physical health. By turning the dial down on our Inner Caveman and turning up our Inner Coach we take a huge step towards living a healthier and happier life.

Getting from noisy Inner Caveman to healthy Inner Coach

If I could travel back in time, I would visit little Zoe in her twenties, give her a massive hug and tell her to hang on in there, because things were about to change for the better. Not only was it socially acceptable to stay in on a Friday night in my thirties, and get up early on a Sunday to get the full use of the day, but it was also the time I discovered my Inner Coach.

My big change started during my counselling training; here I learned I had a choice about how I talked to myself. I know that might sound a bit obvious, but I seriously thought everyone had a version of Brian in their head and that's just how humans were meant to talk to themselves. Understanding I had a choice brought hope that I could leave behind years of overthinking and anxiety. Of course, understanding I had a choice and actually knowing how to change my thinking were very different things. Becoming acquainted with Brian and his favourite types of unhelpful thoughts started the ball rolling, but it wasn't until I learned about the neurological wiring of the human brain that I understood why I got stuck in my thoughts and, more importantly, how to create new ones.

Having got to chapter 8 in this book, you will now have realised I'm not a massive psychobabble fan so, in true Zoe style, I'm going to explain this bit of neuroscience in a nutshell, with the help of Paddy.

Last year we had our garden landscaped by a professional – because I'm now in my forties and that's what I do for fun. But we forgot about Paddy and his squirrel-hunting habit. The day after we had a plethora of beautiful flowers planted, Paddy went into the garden, saw a squirrel and sprinted through the back border, thus creating his very own squirrel path. At first, it took him a while to get through the plants, but over time his unrelenting determination and hatred of squirrels meant he forged a very clear pathway.

This is essentially how we create thoughts. If we think them over and over again then we create a neurological pathway. While this means we may have many of those negative paths in our brain, the good news is, just like Paddy demonstrated, we can create new pathways; it just takes repetition.

As soon as I realised this, I started to become aware of my labelling thought types and began to form new thoughts. To do this, I took a deep breath and I reminded myself that these are labels I learned from others as a child. I accepted that I do make mistakes and, when I do, it doesn't make me an idiot. As I started to form these new thoughts, I noticed I felt different. I didn't have the usual gut punch of shame. Instead, I had a moment of disappointment but then felt empowered; I was in control of my brain.

As time went on, just like Paddy had done in my lovely garden, I created my new pathway, and this became my automatic response. Then there came a time when I realised, "Hang on a second, I haven't called myself an idiot for weeks". I didn't need that old path any more.

Once I saw this change, I started working on my mind reading. I always thought X was thinking Y about me because they gave me a funny look. Being aware of this way of unhelpful thinking meant I could easily spot Brian kicking off. When I realised he was up to his old tricks, I would take myself off for a little wander so that my Inner Coach could objectively look at the evidence. And 99% of the time it declared a simple look could easily mean the person was tired or just happened to be glancing my way. My Inner Caveman, Brian, had made up a story, and by taking myself off for a walk and giving my Inner Coach a moment to check it out, I could see it was irrational. As I did this more, this type of negative, unhelpful thought faded away and new, rational thoughts sprung up.

Then I began to recognise when Brian was about to dismiss a compliment, and instead my Inner Coach encouraged me to say thank you. Admittedly, this felt very uncomfortable at first but again, after a while, I found myself automatically saying thank you and enjoying the compliment. The same happened with celebrating my achievements; Brian would try to minimise them or discount them, but if I took a deep breath and let my Inner Coach fact check him, I uncovered a whole new narrative.

Now I'm in my forties, has Brian left my brain for good? No, the fact is we all need our Inner Cavemen, because they are our bodyguard, and often hero, in life-threatening situations. However, we can develop a much healthier, more rational Inner Coach who is in the driving seat of our brain for most of the time. Over the years, my Inner Coach has become much louder in my head; it's able to take a step back, observe Brian and his stories, do a thorough fact check and then form a more rational perspective. It doesn't pretend I'm amazing, or I don't have any problems; instead, it notices my irrational thoughts and helps form new rational thoughts and pathways.

Knowing I have a choice about how I think, and learning how to stop old patterns, has given me control of my brain and a huge sense of relief. It's allowed me to hush my Inner Caveman, and it's had a monumentally positive effect on my mental, emotional and physical health.

Take some time to imagine what your life would be like with your Inner Coach in control. Would your brain be calmer? How much time would you save by not getting stuck in looping thought? Importantly, what would be the impact on your health?

Your journey to having your own healthy Inner Coach

You are already well on your way to making the journey from noisy Inner Caveman to healthy Inner Coach. By getting to know your Inner Caveman in chapter 2, and becoming aware of its favourite unhelpful thought types, you have taken a huge step forward.

Now you are going to get to know your Inner Coach in its full technicolour glory. You are going to stop letting your survival brain rule the roost and get your thinking brain online. You will bolster this part of your brain's innate wisdom by using the ABC technique to teach it four awesome practices, which will help create these new thoughts and pathways. Throughout the next five chapters, you will build on your Inner Coach's voice to help it guide you through life.

But, first things first, let's meet your healthy Inner Coach.

Exercise 1: Name your Inner Coach

I use the term Inner Coach, but does this work for you? I've heard people refer to this healthy voice as their Inner Wisdom, Inner Counsellor, Higher Self, Best Self or Inner Parent. Some people even give it an actual name. Think about what works for you and feel free to apply this going forward.

Exercise 2: Describe your Inner Coach

Now, what do you want your inner voice to sound like? Calm and collected? Wise like Yoda? (Okay, Yoda maybe not.) All joking aside, the beauty of being able to choose how you speak to yourself means you can literally create your own voice. Take a moment to visualise your Inner Coach and answer these questions:

- What does it look like? An animal, a cartoon character or a human maybe?
- What does it sound like?
- How would you describe its personality?

Examples:
- I call mine my Inner Coach.
- This is the healthiest version of me. It's a cool head in a crisis. It's being able to step back from a situation and respond rather than react.
- It sounds calm and clear-headed, and my own true voice. It engages in rational thoughts and uses facts and evidence to help me make decisions.

- It can be trusted. It's kind and caring but doesn't let me off the hook. It motivates me to push myself but knows my limits. It takes mental, emotional and physical needs seriously and knows the value of self-care.

Exercise 3: Identify your standards

We all have standards for the type of communication we are willing, and not willing, to accept from others. For example, we want kids to be respectful and our partner to be compassionate, and if they don't meet this standard then we know we need to have a conversation with them to challenge the behaviour. Likewise, we need to commit to living up to these standards ourselves. This exercise is all about identifying how you want to talk to yourself going forward and making a commitment from here on in to do just that.

To start you off, take a read through my list of standards.

Examples:
My Inner Coach:
- Is kind and compassionate
- Notices, and challenges, unhelpful types of thoughts
- Is committed to creating rational thoughts
- Uses facts not fiction
- Forms realistic goals and takes responsibility for moving towards those goals
- Accepts mistakes and failures, but tries not to make them

- Views all failures and mistakes as vital feedback, using them as a commitment to learn rather than criticise
- Celebrates successes
- Accepts compliments with a thank you
- Acknowledges I'm an ever-growing human and I have the ability to learn and change
- Has a sensible approach to worrying that analyses risk, makes decisions on what I can control and accepts what I can't

It's not okay for my Inner Coach to:
- Make excuses to let me off the hook or lower my standards
- Be abusive, bully, call me names or berate me in any way

Now it's your turn.

- What do you think about these standards?
- Would they reduce your worrying and negative thinking?
- Are there some changes you want to make?

Take a moment to consider what would work for you and write your own list. Remember, there is no right or wrong, just healthy.

How to unleash your Inner Coach

Now let's use the ABC technique to access your rational brain – your wise and healthy inner voice.

A is for Awareness

Awareness is always the first step to change. This is why in chapter 2 you started to become aware of your Inner Caveman's favourite unhelpful thought types. Take some time to remind yourself of what you discovered.

The next time you witness your Inner Caveman reacting to a situation with an unhelpful negative thought, I want you to move on to step B. Here is a quick reminder of those unhelpful thought types:

1. Labelling: I'm an idiot
2. Mind reading: They think I'm stupid
3. Catastrophising: I've missed the train, so I'm going to lose my job
4. Shoulds: I should be perfect
5. Phoneyism: I'm an imposter
6. Overgeneralising: Everything is terrible
7. Comparison: They have a much better life than me
8. Discounting the positive: I only got the job as no one else applied
9. "What if ...?" thoughts: What if this happens? What if that happens?

B is for Brake

The thinking part of our brain (our Inner Coach) is more active when we are relaxed, which is why we seem to be bursting with wisdom on holiday. Sadly, we can't be on holiday all the time so we need to apply our emergency brake to help us access our thinking brain.

In chapters 9 to 12 I will be introducing you to various ways of distracting your brain and bringing your body under control. First up though, let's recap the techniques you learned in the introduction.

Belly breathing

- Place your hand on your belly
- Breathe deep into your belly for a count of 5, feeling it gently push your hand outwards
- Then breathe out for a count of 7, feeling your hand return

The 5-4-3-2-1 grounding technique

Distracting your five senses:

- LOOK for 5 things you can see around you
- TOUCH 4 things around you or on your body
- LISTEN to 3 sounds around you
- SMELL 2 things around you
- TASTE 1 thing

When you begin to feel calmer, move on to step C.

C is for Coach: How to think like a coach

Your Inner Coach needs to respond to the unhelpful thoughts and create new rational thoughts. To help you do this, I am going to introduce you to four practices:

- Judge and jury
- Helicopter view
- What would Thomas Edison do?
- The Goldilocks approach to worrying

By learning and repeating these simple practices your brain will be creating new rational thoughts and neurological pathways, thus making your Inner Coach your predominant inner voice.

Judge and jury

One of the main roles of our Inner Coach is to challenge our unhelpful thoughts and form more rational thoughts and perspective. As in a courtroom, our Inner Coach can act as judge and jury by reviewing evidence for and against the unhelpful thought and then judging whether it's rational or irrational. In most cases, unhelpful thought types are irrational, because our annoying Inner Caveman has identified one or two pieces of evidence without even bothering to think about the other side or fact check. Next time you notice an unhelpful thought, engage your Inner Coach and follow these instructions:

1. State the evidence for and against the unhelpful thought: what are the facts to back it up and what actually disproves it?
2. Weigh up the evidence for and against and judge if it is a rational or irrational thought.
3. If it's irrational, create a new rational thought to replace the old unhelpful thought.

Example 1:

Situation: Janet had her appraisal and received a mark of excellent in four sections but average in the communication section. Her line manager, David, said her score for communication was lower because she was not speaking up in client meetings. After the appraisal, Janet spent the evening ruminating over losing her job and felt very anxious as a result. Let's explore how the ABC technique helps Janet.

Awareness: Unhelpful thought type
• She spots she is catastrophising

Brake: Deep breathing
• She takes deep breaths to soothe her brain and body

Coach: Her Inner Coach chooses to act as judge and jury
1. Identify the evidence for and against losing job.

Evidence for:
• Average in 20% of her appraisal
• Line manager commented on her not speaking up in meetings

Evidence against:
- In 80% of the appraisal she scored excellent!
- Client feedback shows they are very happy with her approach and the deliverables to date
- Head of the department congratulated her in the lift the other day for this project
- David is pleased with her progress

2. Judge: Little evidence of losing job, so this thought is irrational.
3. Alternative thought: I'm actually doing well. I've achieved a lot over the past year. Next, I need to work on how to speak up in meetings, and David has said he will help me with this.

Example 2:

Situation: Poppy lost out on her dream job. The interview went well but she didn't quite have the experience required. It means she won't get the extra salary and can't apply for the mortgage she wanted. She is 32 and thinks she should own a house by now.

Awareness: Unhelpful thought type
- She spots she is shoulding all over herself again

Brake: 5-4-3-2-1 grounding technique
- She calms herself by using the grounding technique to distract her senses

Coach: Judge and jury
1. Identify the evidence for and against the thought "I should own a house by the age of 32".

Evidence for:
- Her Mum says she should have her own house by now
- Her brother bought a house at 30

Evidence against:
- There is no How to Be an Adult guide that determines the age by which she has to do things
- Most of her friends don't own a house
- Most people her age can't afford a mortgage either unless they are buying with someone else
- Many people never own a house
2. Judge: It doesn't make it true just because her Mum says it!
3. Alternative thought: I would love to own a house but it doesn't matter if it takes time, and it certainly doesn't define me or my worth.

When we challenge our should thoughts we often find the only evidence for them is because someone else said we should. When we take a moment to explore the evidence we quickly find the should thought is irrational. Gaining perspective is imperative to ridding ourselves of the pressure and shame that come with these messages. The more you do this the healthier and happier you will be.

Helicopter view

Here you are going to encourage your wise Inner Coach to get a fresh perspective by zooming out and seeing the bigger picture. Do this by asking:

- Is this a big issue?
- Will this matter to me in a month, a year or five years' time?

Example:

Situation: Cat was on social media flicking through pictures, and started to compare her number of followers (325) to her best friend Jake's 14,563. She ended up calling herself a loser.

Awareness: Unhelpful thought type
- She immediately spots her comparison and labelling thoughts

Brake: Grounding technique
- She puts the brakes on her rising shame by closing down the app and grounding herself

Coach: Helicopter view
- Zoom out: When she takes a step back she acknowledges this isn't a big deal. She knows her social media presence doesn't define her, and her wife and daughter don't love her for her number of followers. She doubts she will care about this in five years' time.
- Inner Coach fresh perspective: I'm getting caught chasing a WoW factor again. I don't need to compare myself with others. I'm worthy no matter how many followers I have!

What would Thomas Edison do?

Thomas Edison famously invented the first working lightbulb after a thousand attempts. Each time he failed, he learned from the experience and tried again until he reached his goal.

We all fail at times and, when we do, we need our Inner Coach to heal our emotional bruises and then motivate us to try again.

Example:
Situation: Liz wants to lead a healthier and more balanced life, which includes eating more varied and nutritious meals. Over the past four weeks, she's been mixing things up in the kitchen and has loved it, but yesterday she was so tired after work she ordered a pizza and ate an entire tub of ice cream, and now she can't stop thinking everything is ruined.

Awareness: Unhelpful thought type
- She recognises she is overgeneralising again

Brake: Distraction
- She puts the brakes on by taking out her phone and looking at pictures of her two kids

Coach: What would Thomas Edison do?
- Inner Coach: Over the past four weeks I've been doing really well. While pizza and ice cream aren't ideal, it's not the end of the world. I know if I get back to

how I would prefer to live in the next day or so then that's more than okay. Sometimes I'm going to fail, and that's to be expected. The aim is to recognise it, learn from it and try again.

The Goldilocks approach to worrying

Goldilocks is a character in a children's story who tastes three bowls of porridge and decides she prefers the one that is just about the right temperature. The concept of just the right amount is one that can really help us if we are chronic worriers. Instead of your Inner Caveman over-worrying and getting caught up in a storm of unhelpful thoughts, let your Inner Coach adopt the Goldilocks approach. The aim is to worry just the right amount; not to the point where you worry so much that you create unnecessary anxiety but enough to adequately risk assess a situation and act accordingly.

To do this, your Inner Coach can ask:

1. What do I know now?
2. What is within my control?
3. What action can I take?

Example:
Situation: Chickenpox is sweeping round the school and Jo is worrying. What if the kids get it ... what if she needs to take time off work ... what if she loses her income for a few weeks ... what if she can't cover the rent ... what if they get evicted?

Awareness: Unhelpful thought type
- "What if …?" game: What if this happens? What if that happens?

Brake: Belly breathing
- 10 deep belly breaths

Coach: Take the Goldilocks approach to worrying
1. What does she know now?
    - There are 22 (of 2000) children off from the school
    - No one in her kids' class has it
    - Her kids have no symptoms
    - She has some savings that can cover them if she can't work
2. What is within her control?
    - She can't stop them catching chickenpox but she can make some plans just in case
3. What action can she take?
    - She can talk to them about following basic hygiene
    - She can make work and her Mum aware of the issue so, if needs be, she can rearrange some of her shifts and ask her Mum to sit

 Take some time here to reflect on these four practices and the examples. Think back to those situations where you have recognised your Inner Caveman getting out of control. Which of these practices would have been helpful to use? What could your Inner Coach have said to you instead?

By taking the time here to do this, you are already forming a new way of thinking and making a commitment to creating those new pathways.

Key aha! moments

Here we are again, another chapter, another set of aha! moments that can help you lead a healthier and happier life. You have created your Inner Coach, and things will never be the same again. In this chapter you learned:

1. We can choose how we speak to ourselves; our Inner Caveman does not have to rule our life.
2. Our Inner Coach is the thinking part of our brain, which uses evidence to provide rational thoughts and gain a rational perspective.
3. Thoughts create neurological pathways in our brain; the more we repeat these thoughts, the stronger the pathway will become.
4. The Inner Coach isn't just about being kind and compassionate; it keeps us accountable for our wellbeing, learns from failure and helps us grow.
5. We can encourage our Inner Coach to become louder by following the ABC technique:

    *   **A** is for Awareness: Recognise unhelpful types of thoughts
    *   **B** is for Brake: Calm your brain so you can access your rational thinking brain (aka your Inner Coach)

- **C** is for Coach: Use this part of your brain to challenge unhelpful thoughts and develop a rational perspective using four practices:
  - Judge and jury: Use evidence to provide rational thoughts
  - Helicopter view: Zoom out and look at the bigger picture
  - What would Thomas Edison do? Learn to face failure and try again
  - The Goldilocks approach to worrying: Just the right amount

CHAPTER 9

From feeling fine to feeling fab

Wear your heart on your sleeve.

PADDY

One of my favourite moments of the day is when I hear the key in the front door, indicating my wife has returned home. For the sake of my relationship, it may be wiser to leave the sentence at that but, I've got to be honest, the best bit is when Paddy greets her. As soon as he hears the key turn, he sprints down the corridor, quicker than when he has seen a squirrel, launches himself in the air while simultaneously wagging his entire body. He then jumps up and down till she strokes him, and he becomes so overcome with excitement that he has to put a shoe in his mouth to calm himself down. It really is quite a sight and, even though I had to do a counselling session barefoot once because he had lost my shoe in the greeting process, this is something that never fails to bring a smile to my face.

If ever there was a species to wear its heart on its sleeve (or fluff), it has to be the dog.

Humans, though, are notoriously a little less on the forthcoming side with their feelings. Men are told that big boys don't cry, us Brits are conditioned to keep a stiff upper lip and don't even get me started on how Londoners view other humans who even dare to make eye contact on the tube, let alone open up about their feelings. Humans have indeed woven a complex web of rules about how we should and shouldn't express our feelings, and it's not doing our species any favours.

Therefore, the question we need to ask is, if holding back our feelings has a negative impact on our wellbeing, is wearing our heart on our sleeve, like Paddy, really the way to go? Honestly, no. Part of the beauty of having a dog is that he doesn't talk. As much as I love him, I don't think I could spend 16 hours a day listening to how excited he is about everything in the entire world (apart from strangers and that Husky in the park). No, I think it's fair to say we all need a filter on our feelings; yes, we need to let them out, but we need to do it safely and in a way with which we feel comfortable.

Whether it's with our best friend, in the counselling room or in a journal, expressing our feelings is cathartic and connects us back to ourselves. Most importantly, we feel lighter, leaving room for those fab feelings like happiness, joy and contentment.

Getting from feeling fine to feeling fab

My favourite story as a child was The Emperor's New Clothes. I used to read it over and over again. The story was about an emperor who was conned by two weavers into buying a very expensive, luxurious but invisible suit. The weavers declared only the stupid and unworthy couldn't see the suit, and the emperor's need for this validation overrode his common sense. When the emperor finally paraded his new clothes in front of his subjects, no one dared to say a word until, finally, a little boy shouted "But he hasn't got anything on!" When I was 6 there was something about that boy shouting the truth that made me feel less tense every time I heard it.

Over 20 years later, I attended my first play therapy training and we were asked to explore our favourite childhood stories. I'd never really thought about it before; I mean, surely I just liked it because of the pretty pictures? However, as each of us shared our favourite stories, we were able to see how the story represented something going on in our little lives at the time and how they helped us express our feelings. As a littleun, I could sense something wasn't right in our house, and that story helped to relieve those uncomfortable feelings even though I was too young to name them. Turns out even when we are little, and our brains don't understand feelings, our feelings need to find a way to come out.

Ever since then, I've always found a good cry at a film or book helps shift some feelings. In my twenties, I used to watch *Titanic* on repeat, which helped but, at three hours a time, it wasn't the most efficient way to get them out. Unfortunately, I hadn't developed many other ways to express feelings, so I would try to comfort them with food or alcohol. I would love to say I realised the error of my ways, had an epic awakening and found the courage to go to counselling, but this wasn't the case. I didn't reach out to anyone, because I found talking about my feelings unbearable. As a child, I learned feelings were scary. People around me didn't know how to express them safely and, when I tried to talk about mine, I was laughed at or my feelings were instantly dismissed or minimised. Therefore, it is no wonder that as an adult I felt far too vulnerable to talk about my feelings.

My path to being a counsellor came about by chance in my late twenties. My insurance job at Canary Wharf wasn't bringing me the success as promised, so I was a tad lost and thought engaging in some voluntary work would be more fulfilling. I chose to work on an LGBT helpline and, to my complete surprise, found myself able to listen, empathise and help people express their feelings. Turns out my parents had given me an unexpected gift; from learning how *not* to have a vulnerable conversation, I knew how to provide a safe space for others.

As much as I saw the value of others sharing their feelings, I still had a deep fear of doing it myself. As I liked the helpline work so much, I enrolled on an introductory counselling course, and it was here we were encouraged to go to counselling ourselves. Don't get me wrong,

I could totally see the value in it, but Brian, my Inner Caveman, was just not having it. He told me I should be able to cope and called me weak for going.

However, if I wanted to be a counsellor, I had to be a client, so I mustered my courage and began the search. I'm not going to lie, I felt very anxious knocking on that door for the first time. I felt uncomfortable in my first session, my second, third and even tenth session. However, over time something changed. I began to trust my counsellor, because when I talked about my feelings she didn't laugh at me or dismiss them; she listened and helped me work through them. This space provided me with way more than a back-to-back session of *Titanic*; it gave me the conditions I needed to explore and express those feelings I had been lugging about with me all through my twenties. Not only was it a massive relief to shed those feelings, but it also taught me how to express my feelings and, crucially, how to find the right people in my life to open up to.

I still find talking about my feelings uncomfortable at times but, whether I'm talking to a counsellor, my very close friends or to myself in a journal, I find getting those feelings out a relief. Don't get me wrong, I still love a good cry at a film while having a nice glass of wine, but I'm much more aware of what I'm feeling and when it's more appropriate to reach for an ear than the remote. The truth is that one way or another your feelings will always find a way to come out. The only choice you have is whether you let them out safely or stuff them down and let them find their own way out. Therefore, being aware of your feelings, and expressing them in the most appropriate way, is the difference between being stuck in feelings and feeling fab.

Your journey to feeling fab

You are already well on your way to feeling fab. By learning how to bring your Inner Caveman under control and giving your Inner Coach permission to speak, you will feel a lot less fear, anger, shame and upset. This means your emotional bucket is going to have more space for those fab feelings.

Of course, that's not to say you aren't going to experience these types of feelings ever again; it's natural to feel them, but it just means there will be fewer of them. When they do show up, I want to help you express them safely. You started this process in chapter 3 by growing your awareness of your emotional bucket and noticing when you were gripped by a feeling or overwhelmed. Sometimes, just by recognising these feelings rather than batting them off, they can start to lose their intensity or even fade away. For those more stubborn feelings, though, you need a different set of tactics.

Exercise: Identify your coping practices

Before we move on to the ABC to help you express those feelings, think about how you currently cope when gripped by a feeling. We all have a go-to set of coping strategies, some of which are healthier than others. Bring awareness to what currently works well and not so well for you so you can build on the good stuff and steer away from the others.

Cast your mind back to the awareness challenge in chapter 3. Here you identified situations where you were either gripped by a feeling or overwhelmed. Can you remember how you reacted? Did you talk to a specific person? Did you watch films, listen to music or hit the gym? What works for you when you feel uncomfortable? What doesn't? Write yourself a list like mine below and let's see what comes up for you.

Zoe's healthy coping practices

- Soppy film when I'm sad
- Counselling when overwhelmed, stuck or grieving
- Talking to my wife
- Listening to some slow music when I feel sad
- Dancing round my bedroom to loud music when I feel scared (it burns off the adrenaline!)
- Mindfulness when I feel overwhelmed
- Boxercise, gym session or yoga
- Cuddling the pooch, walking the pooch, looking at pictures of the pooch

- Writing or drawing
- The iconic Netflix binge

Zoe's not-so-healthy coping practices

- Stuffing them down, pretending they aren't there
- Chocolate, cake, crisps (aka the Carb Fix)
- Wine or beer to take the edge off (aka the Alcohol Fix)
- Snapping at my wife
- Avoiding trigger situations I know will cause uncomfortable feelings
- Hiding under the duvet

As you finish your list, are you surprised by what you uncovered? If you had to pick your most popular unhealthy quick fix, what would it be? Hands down mine is either a carb or alcohol fix. Crisps in the day or a glass of wine to take the edge off at night. It doesn't seem too bad, but the problem is, if I keep grabbing carbs and alcohol, I start to feel a little bit crappy and that defeats the whole reason for grabbing it in the first place.

How to feel fab

Feelings come in all sorts of combinations and intensities, so we need a variety of ways to express them. What works for me might not work for you and vice versa, so here you're going to follow the ABC technique again to help you find your own route to feeling fab.

A is for Awareness

As you know, awareness is always the first step to change, and this is why you explored your feelings in chapter 3. Take some time to remind yourself what you discovered. The next time you encounter one or more of the following feelings, or you notice the signs of feeling overwhelmed, I want you to move on to step B.

- Fear
- Embarrassment
- Guilt
- Shame
- Resentment
- Anger
- Sadness

B is for Brake

When you become aware of a feeling, or a number of feelings swirling around, I want you to apply an emotional emergency brake. When we are consumed with feelings, it can be too uncomfortable to bear, so we often react by reaching for our favourite unhealthy quick fix. If we take a moment to just sit with the feelings and breathe or ground ourselves, we are more likely to choose a healthier way to respond.

Again, try the belly breathing or 5-4-3-2-1 grounding technique. These simple techniques really do pack a calming punch when practised. If you want to experiment with other ways of braking then try these:

- Take a walk for 10, 15 or 20 minutes; getting out of your current environment can give your brain and body the time and space it needs to calm down
- Shift your mood by grabbing your phone and looking at pictures that make you smile
- Distract yourself with a puzzle like a Sudoku, a crossword or a game on your phone

Giving yourself this space will help your Inner Coach respond to the situation.

C is for Coach: How to express your feelings safely

It's your Inner Coach's job to choose the right way for you to express those hard-to-shift feelings. To help it learn how to do this, let's introduce it to the following four practices:

- Using motion to shift emotion
- Expressing feelings through writing
- Embracing The Beatles: Get a little help from your friends
- Embracing The Beatles: Help, I need somebody

Using motion to shift emotion

Motion is an excellent emotion shifter. Take fear, for example. We have learned when we experience fear that our body wants us to run away or fight, so moving our body literally provides it with what it needs to feel safe. Don't worry, this isn't the you must exercise three times a week lecture; this is about helping you identify ways of moving your body to shift feelings. Ten minutes of stretching your body after a nice shower, or going for a walk and taking some deep breaths, can make a huge difference to how you feel.

When I'm feeling overwhelmed, just getting out of the house for a walk feels hard enough, but this mini achievement, combined with the motion and connection to nature, really helps change my feelings. However, if I'm feeling frustrated or angry, I need a different type of movement to shift my high energy, so I take a boxercise class or go for a fast walk. When I'm feeling sad, I prefer a gentle yoga class or a slow walk with the dog.

 Are you aware of what types of movement help shift your mood? Does a cardio session shift those feelings? Does dancing around the bedroom to your favourite tunes help lift your energy? What effect does a walk at lunchtime have during a busy workday? If you don't know the answers to these questions then I invite you to experiment with motion and find the movements that work for you.

By being aware of your feelings, and the types of motion that help shift your emotions, you will be able to control your feelings, rather than your feelings controlling you.

Expressive writing

Whether it is writing a diary as a teenager, keeping a journal as an adult or just letting rip with pen and paper when the mood takes us, writing has been providing instant relief for humans for centuries.

If you have been sceptical of this form of expression then listen to the research. In the late 1980s James W. Pennebaker, a social psychologist from the University of Texas, conducted a now infamous study where participants spent 15 minutes a day writing for four days in a row. The results were clear: this activity significantly reduced their feelings of distress and led to fewer visits to health centres. There have been numerous studies since then that have shown the same thing, and I too have seen many clients benefit from writing their heart out. If you want to add this to your arsenal of practices then I would suggest experimenting with the following.

Expressive writing for overwhelm
Instructions:
- Find a place where you will not be disturbed and write for up to 15 minutes
- Just write; don't worry about your handwriting, spelling or grammar, just get those words on the page and don't stop till those 15 minutes are up

- When you have finished, don't read it back but just put it somewhere safe
- If you try this for at least four days consecutively then you will feel your emotional bucket drain to a more manageable level

Journaling when gripped by a feeling

Journaling is cathartic. It takes the feeling from inside you and places it safely on the page. Giving yourself the time to explore these feelings is a gift to yourself. Not only will it bring more awareness to why you are feeling a certain way but it will also lead to a great sense of relief.

You don't need the perfect notebook or beautiful handwriting. It doesn't have to be an essay or an expletive-free zone. Try experimenting; journal when you are gripped by a feeling, or take a more proactive approach and keep your emotional bucket light by journaling every day. Alternatively, use this method to enhance your learning by journaling as you read a book (hint hint) or between counselling sessions.

Embracing The Beatles: Get a little help from your friends

Beware the beer commercial or TV soap that shows a person with a million best friends, for all relationships are not equal. Whether it's with an old school friend, a sibling or someone we've just met at work, relationships differ massively. Some relationships we can rely on for fun and others for a good debate; but there are only ever a few people – and by this I mean one or two, if you are very fortunate – to whom we can truly open up. Working out who these people are is central to meeting our emotional needs.

Who are those few people in your life you feel able to open up to? If you are struggling with this, think about the people who:

- *Listen without jumping in with their own stuff or checking their phone every two minutes*
- *Keep your confidentiality*
- *Empathise with you rather than saying "Get over it" or "Oh well, at least you have ..." or some other equally trite response*
- *Don't minimise, laugh at or dismiss your feelings*

How often do you reach out to them? How often do they reach out to you? If it's not very often then what's getting in the way? Do you need to take a leap of faith and reach out more? Would arranging some more quality time together help deepen the relationship?

By investing in these rich relationships, we give ourselves a deeper connection to the person, and it provides us with that safe space when we really need it.

Example:

Situation: Colin applied for six jobs and didn't get one interview. He is demotivated at work and missing his daughter, who recently moved out.

Awareness: Gripped by overwhelm

- Feelings: Feeling full, intense low mood.
- Thoughts: Looping, overgeneralising.
- Physical sensations: Tense, tired and difficulty sleeping.
- Behaviour: Eating more, withdrawing more.

Brake:

- He can feel the fear rising in his body, and he wants to raid the fridge for goodies. Instead he takes three long, deep breaths and thinks about who he can reach out to.

Coach:

- He hasn't spoken to Alison for ages, but she is always really helpful to talk to, so he texts her "Hi Alison, are you around this week for a catch-up? I've not been feeling myself recently and I could do with a chat."

Reaching out can feel vulnerable, but if you can identify someone you trust then it is one of the best ways of helping you express those feelings.

Embracing The Beatles: Help, I need somebody

When reaching out to friends or family seems too vulnerable, or isn't shifting the overwhelm or those lingering feelings, reaching out to a helpline or counsellor may be more effective. Professional help isn't tea and sympathy; it's being in a safe place with someone who has a huge amount of training and experience. They are not going to judge you or tell you what to do; they are 100% there to support you. I feel incredibly honoured when someone sits with me and expresses their feelings. It takes a huge amount of courage, and it really is one of the most effective ways to express those more stubborn feelings.

If you want to try private counselling, I would suggest meeting two or three therapists and seeing how you feel with them. Counselling is an investment, as it takes time, money and energy, so make sure you find the right counsellor for you.

 Now we have explored these four practices, take some time to reflect on:

- *Which of these do you think will help you in your journey to feeling fab?*
- *How can you incorporate them into your life?*

Integrating these into your life is the difference between feeling far from fine and feeling fab, so start experimenting with your ABC and find what really works for you.

Key aha! moments

Feelings, eh? We can't outrun them no matter how hard we try; however, we can learn to express them safely. In this chapter you learned:

1. Wearing our heart on our sleeve is not a safe way to express our feelings. We all need to find our own way.
2. Our feelings will find a way to come out, so we must either control them or they will control us.
3. By turning down the volume on your Inner Caveman and turning up your Inner Coach you will automatically be creating less shame, guilt, fear, anger and upset, but that doesn't mean you won't ever experience these feelings again.
4. When we recognise we are gripped by feelings or are overwhelmed we can take back control by using the ABC technique:
   - **A** is for Awareness: Recognise when you are gripped by a feeling or overwhelmed
   - **B** is for Brake: Calm your brain and body so you don't react in old unhealthy ways
   - **C** is for Coach yourself: Express your feelings safely by using one of the following practices:
     - Using motion to shift emotion
     - Expressing feelings through writing
     - Embracing The Beatles: Get a little help from your friends
     - Embracing The Beatles: Help, I need somebody (helpline or counselling)

CHAPTER 10

From anxious state to calm state

People are too complicated to have simple labels.

PHILIP PULLMAN

A world without labels would be a confusing place. Seriously, no one wants to spend five hours in the supermarket trying to distinguish the contents of a can of meatballs from dog food, or playing Russian roulette with an edible plant and a poisonous one. Yes, there is definitely a place in the world for a label; it can keep us safe, save us time and provide us with much-needed clarity. When it comes to humans, I think labelling gets trickier. Are labels helpful when we talk about anxiety?

Take Paddy. He becomes anxious around strangers and has been like this ever since we picked him up at the age of 8 weeks old. The first 16 weeks of a dog's life are incredibly important as that's their window of opportunity to get used to the world. Unfortunately, for neither love nor money, and despite a significant amount of my blood, sweat and tears, could we teach Paddy to be calm around strangers.

Then the teacher at puppy school suggested we bought him a jacket with the label "Nervous". This was helpful because people avoided stroking him, but it was also unhelpful as people assumed he was scared of everything so kept their dogs away, meaning he missed out on his much-loved playtime. Labelling him took away the situations that caused him to feel anxious but also took away a lot of what he could do and enjoyed.

When people label themselves as an anxious person then it can do more harm than good. Of course, being aware of feeling anxious can help us access specific help, but it is incredibly disempowering if we see it as a fixed part of our identity. As you learned in previous chapters, anxiety is caused by our brain, body and unexpressed feelings. At my worst, my brain tried to eat itself up so much that I wasn't sure if I would ever have a rational thought again, and then my body would pitch in with a cocktail of feelings and hormones that made me want to crawl out of my skin. Sometimes I thought this was just how I was meant to be.

Turns out that way of thinking was part of the problem; labelling myself as an anxious person was not only incredibly disempowering, it was also untrue. I've learned that anxiety is not a disease I have; it is a *dis-ease* that sits in my brain and body and, most importantly, it's something that I can control and ease.

Dogs may not be able to change much, but us humans can, so I say let's leave the labels for cans in the supermarket. Have you given yourself a label? How does ditching the label and taking back control sound? I found it a massive relief, and that's how I want you to feel too.

Getting from anxious to calm

My first steps to taking back control were forming my Inner Coach voice and letting my feelings out; that's why the chapters that help you to do this too precede this one. Getting these practices down meant I had more control over my survival brain and that well-meaning but ridiculously behaved Inner Caveman. As I recognised my unhelpful thoughts and engaged my Inner Coach, I noticed I was triggering my body less, leading to less anxiety. Coupled with learning how to acknowledge and express my feelings, rather than trapping them inside, this helped my body feel more at ease. However, it didn't completely slay the beast. The final piece of the puzzle was to learn how to lead a balanced life.

Integrating calm into my busy life was a challenge to begin with. In theory, I had always understood that this self-care malarkey everyone was going on about was a good thing but, on a practical level, I never fully embraced it. In my family and culture, self-care was deemed self-indulgent and for other people who had nothing better to do. Meditation and yoga were for hippies, and self-care was a bath on a Sunday evening. Hard work, however, was much more valued and deemed a sure sign of success. Therefore, even though I knew taking time out was good for my brain, and the anxiety, I just didn't value it. It wasn't until I completed the exercise in chapter 4 – of looking at my hectic routine and noticing all the activities that threw my body in and out of anxiety – that I realised how much pressure my body was under. No wonder my migraines brought me to a standstill each month. It was my body's way of getting me to rest and reset.

When I finally began to see the value in looking after my brain and body, I started to slowly reduce some of the anxiety-inducing activities in my week and introduce some small moments of calm. This made a difference, but it still didn't bring consistent balance into my life. It wasn't until I started to really question my thinking about productivity and self-care that I was able to make significant long-term changes. During this exploration with my counsellor I realised how many shoulds I had internalised about working hard, often thinking I was lazy or worthless if I took time out for self-care. Once I realised it was Brian doing this, I began to challenge those irrational shoulds. As a result, I was able to give myself permission to embrace self-care. I started by planning out my week in advance; I'd grab a whiteboard and schedule in much-needed rest and recuperation.

Limiting those anxiety-inducing activities, and scheduling calming activities, not only stopped me walking around in a cloud of anxiety but also helped me reset. My body no longer felt the need to give me migraines because I gave it what it needed.

Of course, just because I had written my schedule on a whiteboard didn't mean my life went to plan. So, when I noticed my anxiety begin to surge, I learned how to apply an emergency brake and reduce it in the moment. I'm not going to say I now live the serene life of a monk on a hillside in the Himalayas but, by channelling my Inner Coach and managing my lifestyle, I live a much calmer life, and my body is more at ease.

Your journey to calm

By investing time in growing your Inner Coach and learning how to express your feelings, you will hopefully quickly notice that you feel less anxious. Now it's time for you to bring even more balance to your life, and I'll help you do this. Let's start by reminding you of your work in chapter 4. You took a step back and observed your routine and made some small adjustments. To build on this let's free you from your irrational thinking on productivity and self-care so you can introduce even more calming activities into your life.

Many of us struggle to integrate calm into our lives, because we have formed some unhealthy thoughts about our productivity levels. This way of thinking is very common because we are bombarded with should messages about working hard from an early age. Our families may have encouraged us to work hard and push on through, even when we are sick. Our schools, colleges and universities may have told us we should work hard, and our culture sends us constant messages about how we should be working long hours to be deemed successful. These messages promote living a busy lifestyle, with the promise of success and worthiness, but in reality it often only delivers exhaustion and anxiety.

Exercise 1: The productivity trap

Let's take a moment to explore your shoulds about productivity. When you read these questions, what comes up for you?

- What's your attitude towards productivity?
- Do you feel guilt or even shame when you take time out for self-care?
- Do you think you have to be productive all the time to be successful?

Based on your answers, can you identify your should thoughts about productivity and self-care? If you find this difficult, here are the common shoulds I've encountered in the counselling room. Do the following sound familiar to you?

- I should be productive all the time
- I shouldn't take time out for self-care as it's lazy
- I should work long hours to be successful

In chapter 8 you learned how to challenge this type of unhelpful thought using the ABC technique, so let's see what that learning looks like in practice by considering an example situation.

Example:
Situation: It's Sunday afternoon and Bella has a long list of chores and a report she needs to read before her first meeting tomorrow. She is still shattered from last week but just can't relax because she keeps thinking "I should be doing something productive".

Awareness: Unhelpful thought type
• Bella notices her should thought

Brake: Deep belly breathing
• She takes 10 long, deep belly breaths

Coach: Use the judge and jury practice to challenge the thought
1. Identify the evidence for and against "I should be doing something productive":

   Evidence for:
   • She has lots of tasks that need doing
   • She thinks about her Mum, who never rested on a Sunday and she had a job and three kids and always had a tidy house!

   Evidence against:
   • She is shattered

- Her work rate is plummeting during the week as she is so tired
- Her busy life is starting to affect her motivation levels
- She has been feeling low all week
- She is at risk of burnout again if she doesn't rest
- Her brain and body need rest

2. Judge: She can see this should thought is irrational and really unhelpful for her wellbeing.
3. Alternative thought: I like to be productive but I know I need some self-care today. Just because Mum did this doesn't mean I should too. We are different and that's okay.

If you live by your productivity shoulds, you are creating lots of unnecessary anxiety and not valuing or prioritising the time your brain and body need to rest and recuperate. The aim of challenging your should thoughts isn't to stop you being productive; it's to give your brain and body what they need to rest and make you more efficient. I know it sounds counterintuitive but, by easing off the accelerator, you can reduce your anxiety and be much more productive. To embrace this new way of thinking, I want you to give yourself permission to incorporate some calming practices into your life. Change your shoulds to:

- I like to be productive but I also value downtime, so I give myself permission to rest
- I like to be productive but my worth isn't dependent on this
- I like to be productive and self-care helps me reset and rest

How does this sound to you? Are you willing to make this commitment so you can take the next step towards shedding your anxiety and living in a calmer state?

Exercise 2: Finding balance

Now you are aware of the productivity trap, let's bring some more balance into your life. Look back at chapter 4; are you still engaging in too many of those anxiety-inducing activities? If so, spend some time now planning your up-and-coming week.

- Which activities can you limit, in order to help reduce your anxiety?
- Do you have enough activities in your week to induce a sense of calm?

If you are struggling to identify calming activities, here are some of the common ways to provide quick and effective relief from anxiety. Now, before you say "Oh no, not the sleep, hydrate, eat speech", hear me out on how they have a positive impact on anxiety.

Sleep

Oh sleep, how I love thee. When we sleep, we press reset on our brain and body. As each of us is unique we all need different amounts of sleep. I love nine hours, and my other half functions like a queen on seven hours. Brian, my Inner Caveman, used to compare us and call me lazy, but I've realised not all bodies are built equally. I need what I need, and she needs what she needs, end of story. Getting the right amount of sleep, as often as we can, is a massive factor in keeping anxiety at bay. Sleep also has a huge impact on how our Inner Coach functions. If we don't get enough sleep we tend to function more with our survival brain, leaving our Inner Caveman to whip up even more anxiety.

Be honest with yourself: how much sleep helps your Inner Coach be on top form? How does a lack of sleep contribute to your daily anxiety levels?

Water

Hydration is important for a few reasons. Dehydration may cause some people to experience body sensations that are similar to anxiety. This is especially true in the morning; it is possible to wake up feeling anxious, and this can be caused by dehydration.

Secondly, our brain is about 73% water, so if you don't give it what it needs, your body is going to become stressed, and you can bet it will let you know in an unpleasant way that it's not happy.

How much water have you been drinking over the past few days? Do you wake up and drink a glass of water or grab a coffee instead? Simple changes of habit can all add up to make a significant difference to our state.

Food and drinks

Our relationship with food and drinks can often be complex for many reasons, and this topic deserves a book in its own right. I don't profess to be an expert in this field but there are a few useful observations I can make about the link between food, drinks and anxiety. Firstly, being hungry can mimic anxiety sensations in the body, so we may feel anxious when we wake up or when we skip meals. Having regular meals, planning these in advance and carrying around healthy snacks can help us maintain our energy levels and give our brain and body what they need.

Secondly, I'm sad to announce that too much caffeine can also create body sensations that mimic anxiety. Now, I don't want to take away your beloved morning coffee, but I want you to be aware of how it makes you feel. I know if I have more than one coffee in a day my heart will pump a little faster and I will not feel at ease. As I've said many times, we are all different and this goes for our tolerances of food and caffeine too. My advice is to experiment; get to know your body by trying different foods and monitoring how they affect your anxiety.

Thirdly, you are aware from reading this book that I have a comfort eating and drinking coping mechanism. I know I haven't been paying attention to my needs if I find myself staring into the cupboard looking for carbs or grabbing a large glass of wine to take the edge off the day. I know it's a sign there is *dis-ease* in my brain and body. I then

179

have a choice: I can call on the ABC technique to help me, or I can devour a bag of crisps. Reader, I'm not going to lie, occasionally I still choose crisps. However, when this happens, I engage my Inner Coach and I don't beat myself up. Instead, I have a good long sleep and the next day I explore why I found myself needing those crisps. I then do something to help myself. The key to living a balanced life isn't getting it right all the time; it's getting yourself back on track when you need to.

Holistic treatments

As we saw in chapter 4, anxiety can cause tension in our muscles. Frequent aches and pains are the body's way of telling us to slow down. There are many holistic treatments, from the traditional massage to Reiki, which can help shift tension and energy blocks in our body.

If a hot stones session sounds a bit out there to you, how do you know it is until you try? Plan in some sort of treatment once a month to give your body what it needs. Again, making space for these small changes can help your body live in the peace it deserves.

Downtime (time out)

Valuing and prioritising downtime regularly can make a massive difference to your levels of anxiety. Committing to one or all of these can help you reduce your anxiety throughout the day:

- Don't look at your phone till you are showered and dressed in the morning and stop looking at least 30 minutes before you go to sleep
- Get up 20 minutes earlier and have a relaxed breakfast instead of rushing off
- Take a walk at lunchtime and break up the day
- Get off the bus a stop earlier and walk the last 10 minutes to your destination
- Treat yourself; have tea and cake and relax
- Snuggle on the sofa and read a chapter of that book you started last month

As you can see, you don't need to enrol on an epic retreat to recharge. A simple 10 minutes out here and there during the day can be enough to reset.

Transition times

I think of transition times as offering a circuit breaker for anxiety. Commuting, gaps between meetings or those five minutes during ad breaks on TV are all times where we can choose to wind ourselves up or wind ourselves down. Being more conscious of these transition moments during the day can make a big difference to our anxiety levels. Use them to relax, be mindful or visualise the day going well. Nurture yourself with music or a crossword or listen to a funny podcast. Consider not grabbing your phone and overloading your brain with more information. Use the time to switch off and give yourself some time to be.

Connection

As social animals, we all need to connect with others. Too little and we can feel lonely, and too much and we can feel overwhelmed. Remember, we are all different, so what I need may be different to what you need. As an introvert, I need lots of time to re-energise after socialising. To create this balance my Inner Coach has learned to plan in some time to myself around social engagements. I especially do this around big parties or family gatherings, which take a lot of energy. Taking this approach has been instrumental in managing my anxiety levels. I don't always get the balance right, but by paying attention to my needs I can adjust my socialising as necessary. Identifying what you need and planning around this can help you lead that balanced life.

Mindfulness

I often think of mindfulness as a bath for the brain. It gives us a break from our noisy inner lives and brings a sense of calm within. There are a huge number of books dedicated to mindfulness so I won't go into too much detail about this practice. However, what I would say is that mindfulness is a little bit like exercise. Firstly, there are many types so you may need to experiment before you find the right one for you. Secondly, if you haven't practised before, it can take time to build up those muscles. If you started running tomorrow it would take a while to build up to running a 5k. The same applies to mindfulness; building up to a whole hour takes time. My advice is to join a group or listen to various exercises on the likes of YouTube. Whatever you do, start off slowly and see if this can be something you integrate into your week.

 Before you move on, reflect on these calming activities and identify three that you could incorporate into your coming week. Try experimenting next week too and see what works for you.

How to relieve anxiety in the moment

We know we feel anxiety in our body as a response to a perceived threat. When we ignore this physical response, we feed our anxiety. By paying attention to our body sensations, we can notice our anxiety rise and then bring it back under control. As ever, you are going to use the ABC technique to equip your Inner Coach with the practices it needs to help you.

A is for Awareness

In chapter 4 you started to become aware of how anxiety manifests in your body. The next time you notice one of the tell-tale body sensations that your anxiety levels are rising, I want you to move on to step B.

1. Uncomfortable, fast heartbeat
2. Short, quick breaths into your chest
3. Stomach churning or fluttering, often called butterflies, leading you to need the loo more

4. Tensed muscles
5. Difficulty concentrating and poor memory
6. Sweaty, with heat creeping up your body
7. Nauseous
8. Wobbly legs
9. Dry mouth, difficulty in swallowing
10. Wide, dilated eyes

B is for Brake

These body sensations can be very uncomfortable and it can be tempting to react by reaching for your go-to quick fix. If you take a moment to just sit with the body sensations and breathe, you are more likely to choose a healthier way to bring your anxiety under control.

C is for Coach: How to relieve anxiety

Now is the time for your Inner Coach to learn how to respond to anxiety surges in the moment. Here are two options to help you do this:
• Apply the Anxiety First Aid Kit
• Challenge thoughts or express feelings

Apply the Anxiety First Aid Kit

When our anxiety is triggered and about to run roughshod over our day, it's helpful to have some go-to practices that can bring us back into a calm state. I like to call this my trusty Anxiety First Aid Kit. Instead of plasters and bandages, this kit is made up of quick practices that swiftly help distract our brain and body, taking us out of anxiety and into a calmer state. Sometimes all we need to do to help ourselves in the moment is to choose one of these practices.

The good news is that you have been experimenting with many of these already. So far, you have tried distracting your brain and soothing your body by:

- Belly breathing
- 5-4-3-2-1 grounding technique
- Taking a walk
- Looking at pictures of loved ones
- Solving puzzles

The Anxiety First Aid Kit includes two more practices:

Mindfulness

Being mindful – or paying attention, as I prefer to call it – doesn't have to be an hour-long session. Simply turning our attention to one thing for three minutes can distract our Inner Caveman from kicking up fear. Try listening to an entire song on the train in the morning or taking a few minutes at lunchtime to sit on a bench and focus on the sounds around you. By committing to giving yourself three minutes to focus, you can learn to quieten your mind.

Stretching

Whenever Paddy wakes up from a snooze, he throws out the most perfect downward-facing dog pose. We humans also need to stretch and by engaging in three minutes of yoga or some simple stretches, you can give your body what it needs and induce a state of calm.

Challenging thoughts or expressing feelings

You can also reduce anxiety by using the ABC techniques and practices from the previous two chapters.

• Check in with your thoughts:

Are you creating unnecessary anxiety by getting caught up in unhelpful thoughts again? Is your Inner Caveman catastrophising? Is it incessantly worrying or comparing? If so, go back to chapter 8 and start to work through your ABC technique. Remember, new healthy neurological pathways (healthy rational thoughts) take time to create, so don't be disheartened if this is the cause of the *dis-ease*. Challenge those thoughts, find that rational perspective and take back control, and as you do you will start to feel the anxiety subside.

• Check in with your feelings:

Are you overwhelmed or gripped by feelings? If so, find a way to express those feelings. Grab your journal or pick up the phone and arrange to meet your trusted friend. If those feelings still won't shift, call a helpline or start the process of finding a counsellor in your area. Taking action means you are taking back control from anxiety. Don't forget, these ABC techniques take time to learn and integrate into your everyday life, so don't be discouraged if you have to go back to previous chapters and do some more reflecting. Remember, we are all works in progress and this book is your pocket guide for life.

Key aha! moments

Anxiety sucks, but you have learned a huge amount about how it works in the body, as well as understanding how to control it. Here are your aha! moments:

1. An anxiety label can help us access specific help, but it can also be disempowering if we think this is just how we are meant to be.
2. Anxiety is a *dis-ease* that sits in our brain and body and, most importantly, it's something that we can control and ease.
3. By using our Inner Coach as our main voice and expressing our feelings, we can feel less anxious.
4. Our unhelpful thoughts about productivity can keep us stuck in a hectic lifestyle and in an anxious state.
5. Giving ourselves permission for self-care can make us more productive as we are less anxious and more efficient.
6. We can create a balanced life by incorporating: sleep, water, regular food, holistic treatments, downtime, transition-friendly times, connection and mindfulness.
7. We learned how to relieve anxiety in the moment by using the ABC technique:
    - **A** is for Awareness: Notice uncomfortable body sensations

- **B** is for Brake so you don't react by reaching for old unhealthy ways of coping
- **C** is for Coach: Respond by using the Anxiety First Aid Kit:
    - Belly breathing
    - 5-4-3-2-1 grounding technique
    - Taking a walk
    - Looking at pictures of loved ones
    - Solving puzzles
    - Mindfulness
    - Stretching

and

By checking in with your thoughts and feelings!

CHAPTER 11

From pleasing to assertive action

Put your own oxygen mask on first.

EVERY FLIGHT, EVERY DAY

We all know the drill; you're sat on a plane, about to fly off an hour later than planned because buying the cheaper airline ticket seemed a good idea at the time, when the air attendant launches into the safety briefing. It's the usual spiel: seat belt fastened, stay seated till the sign goes off, life jacket blah blah blah. Part of me thinks they could skip this bit and make back 10 minutes of the delay, but then they come to the oxygen mask bit, and I'm always mesmerised: "If the air pressure drops, please ensure you put your own oxygen mask on first, before helping others."

I know great poets and literary giants of the world may not agree with me on this, but I think the oxygen mask spiel is nothing short of profound, as it is the perfect metaphor for those of us with people-pleasing tendencies. The message is clear: if you don't put your needs first then you won't be able to help others, plus you might die.

Okay, so that's a tiny bit over the top, but there's truth in it. You may be able to get away with helping your holiday buddy for a minute or so, but it's not going to be long before you are passed out on the floor, helping precisely no one. This is the same in life; if we don't look after our needs and act assertively then, sooner or later, we will not be in a fit state to help ourselves, let alone anybody else.

Of course, context is king; if the oxygen masks do come down then you can bet your bottom dollar it's for a pretty serious reason, so we don't overthink it or feel guilty, we just do it. In everyday life, though, the path to getting our needs met by taking assertive action is much more complex. As you learned in chapter 1, we have many needs, and they can change on a daily basis. For example, I know if I get only a few hours' sleep then this severely affects me the next day. Like the day after I was up all night with a sick Paddy, who was howling like a baby wolf because, in his infinite wisdom, he had decided to eat a snail. My lack of sleep meant my physical energy was depleted, mentally I was struggling to access my Inner Coach, and I felt scared and a tiny bit angry at the little monkey. When my needs are not being met like this then what I say yes or no to, and the decisions I make that day, will *need* to be different to those I made the day before.

Even when our needs are met, and we are feeling fab, we can still find it difficult to take assertive action. How can you visit Great Auntie Sue and say no to a piece of her trifle that she has made especially for you? You know if you eat it, your lactose intolerance will leave you in pain for the rest of the day; but, on the other hand, can you tolerate the guilt and her disappointed face? For many, the emotional discomfort from disappointing someone can stop them dead in their assertive tracks.

It's fair to say that setting boundaries (or saying no) may not be a familiar path for many of us. But, once we understand the steps we need to take, it often becomes one of the most worthwhile journeys of all.

Getting from people-pleasing to taking assertive action

Before I show you how to take assertive action, we need to talk about your expectations. This is not a once-in-a-lifetime journey; this is a path you have to take every day. Sometimes you will bounce along with it like Tigger on a hot summer's day, and other times you will become completely and utterly lost. For example, on Thursday you may say no to baking a cake for the school summer fete, give Jim that difficult feedback and calmly communicate a clear set of boundaries to your teenage son. However, on Friday you may say yes to babysitting when you know you need to look after yourself, and you back down on that boundary you were so proud of setting the day before. Building our assertive muscles takes time, and this is when we need our Inner Coach to help us out by celebrating when we nail it and learning from when we fail at it.

It would also be remiss of me not to acknowledge how some of the journeys will be way more complex than putting on an oxygen mask or saying no to a piece of cake. Halfway down the path, you are going to feel the urge to give up and turn back. My advice here is stick with it, because the destination is always worth it. Let me give you a few examples.

In my twenties, I decided it was time to come out to my family. I was fed up with living a life of shoulds as it was affecting my mental, emotional and physical wellbeing. I wanted them to know the real me and be part of my life. You know when you hear those heart-warming stories of parents turning around and saying "It doesn't matter. I love you just the way you are"? Well, my experience was nothing like that. The response from my Dad was "I don't want to know" and I was promptly told to leave. In the months that followed, I received many texts and letters trying to persuade me from my "choice". Initially, I hoped it was just a knee-jerk reaction, but when the letters started demanding I marry a man to make them proud, I quickly lost hope.

When someone's behaviour has a negative impact on our physical, emotional or mental health, we have a choice about how we respond. We can deprioritise our needs, people-please and let the behaviour continue, be aggressive and shout and scream back, or we can set a healthy boundary. Despite wanting to shout and scream back, I decided I needed to put on my oxygen mask and set a boundary. My boundary was this: it's acceptable to not like my sexuality, but it's not acceptable to be judgemental or abusive; if these letters continue I will walk away. Unfortunately, my boundary was ignored and the abuse continued, so I had a new decision to make. I had to either follow through with my boundary or let the abuse continue. Even though I didn't want to lose my parents, I had to prioritise my mental and emotional health and I stopped contact.

It wasn't until four years later that my Dad reached out via text message. It wasn't a gushing apology and didn't acknowledge the four-year gap, but it was respectful. It took a further six years for my parents to meet my now wife. They didn't attend our wedding, and they won't visit our home, but they are respectful of the boundary I set all those years ago. The relationship is far from how I would like it to be but it is a lot healthier for all of us, and I dread to think where I would be in life if I had continued to put their needs before mine. Putting on our own oxygen mask in life can be far from easy, but sometimes it's literally a lifesaver.

You would think, having formed the ability to take assertive action in the big moments in life, that the little moments would be a breeze to me. Unfortunately, in 2016 let's just say I took my eye off the ball. I followed the classic burnout formula. I looked after everyone else's needs, worked too many hours and ignored the signs; I was far from fine and found myself suffering. My needs became so neglected that even getting up and dressed felt like swimming through treacle. I had no choice but to take some time out. I went to see my ever-patient counsellor and moaned about how it was everybody else's fault: "They gave me too much work", "They didn't listen when I said no" blah blah blah. I was fuelled by anger and blame but, when I ran out of steam, I had to face the inescapable truth that I was responsible for my own needs. Gently, my counsellor helped me acknowledge some of my less-than-helpful behaviours, and that's when the true extent of my small moments of people-pleasing behaviour was revealed.

I tell you my story to show you the twists and turns of the epic adventure, which is the journey from people-pleasing to assertive action. Some days you will crack it and take 10 steps forward, and on others you may take two steps back. It's not easy, but I can assure you I have never regretted taking assertive action, and every day I live a much healthier life because of it.

 Now you have read my story, please stop and take a few moments to reflect on yours. When have you been proud of the boundaries you've set? When have you said no and felt a huge sense of relief? Would you like to do this more? If so, you are going along the right path!

Your journey to assertive action

By engaging in reflection exercises over the previous three chapters you have already started to focus on your needs and are well on the way towards growing those assertive muscles:

- By cultivating your Inner Coach you are committing to looking after your mental health needs
- By expressing your feelings you are committing to looking after your emotional needs
- By learning how to bring yourself into a calm state you are committing to looking after your physical needs

As I said in chapter 5, your needs matter because you matter, so paying attention to your needs is a fantastic step towards living a healthier and happier life. This doesn't mean you are a selfish person or that you can't be kind and do nice things for other people. You are just ensuring that you are kind to yourself too and get what you need.

Once you learn the habit of taking assertive action, you can start to confidently get your needs met without being fearful of the reaction from others or feeling guilty. As time goes on, your assertive muscles will grow, and you will feel lighter and more in control of your actions and, ultimately, your life. Now, who wouldn't want that, eh?

Defining assertive action

Before you move on to the ABC of how to take assertive action, let's get clear what it actually means. In the context of human needs, I define assertive action as:

The ability to identify and communicate our needs in an appropriate, clear and respectful manner.

Assertive action is *not*:

- **Passive**: This is where we take no action at all and avoid communicating our needs.
- **Passive-aggressive**: Expecting people to know or guess what we need and then feeling angry when they don't deliver. Our communication is often unclear and can be sarcastic.
- **Aggressive**: Here we communicate our needs through demanding, forceful or threatening language or actions.

While I have engaged in all of these behaviours, I would say being a passive queen used to be my default position. Take some time here to think about how you typically get your needs met. By being aware of your go-to behaviours, you can stop reacting in old unhealthy ways and choose a healthy assertive response instead.

How to take assertive action

Taking assertive action may be tricky but it is very much a skill your Inner Coach can master over time. To learn this skill, you are going to call on the trusty ABC technique again.

A is for Awareness

In chapter 5 I told you about our most prevalent people-pleasing behaviours:

1. Saying yes when we need to say no
2. Avoiding conflict like the plague
3. Avoiding giving feedback or an opinion
4. Difficulty in setting boundaries or maintaining boundaries
5. Difficulty in making decisions involving others
6. Being a great listener and empathic but tending to do this too much for others
7. Finding being assertive difficult
8. Putting tasks for others before self-caring

The next time you become aware that you are about to fall back into your people-pleasing ways, I want you to move to step B.

B is for Brake

Odds are, if you are in a situation where you are faced with the decision to either people-please or take assertive action, your brain and body are going to be experiencing a rush of anxiety. To bring your brain and body back under control, and override the strong urge to people-please, you need to give yourself a break. Researcher and storyteller Brené Brown, who is my go-to personal development guru when I need some wisdom, breathes and twists a ring on her finger three times before she responds to any requests. As she does this her internal mantra is "Choose discomfort over resentment". Creating a ritual helps put the brake on your anxiety; it also provides an opportunity to ground yourself. Whether you use this practice or any of the others from your Anxiety First Aid Kit, this moment of calm will provide you with the opportunity to choose your response rather than reacting passively or aggressively.

C is for Coach: How to manage your needs and take assertive action

Your wise Inner Coach can help you take assertive action by always remembering these three steps:

1. Identify your needs
2. Communicate your needs
3. Protect your needs

Step 1: Identify your needs

Firstly, you need to be able to identify and prioritise your needs. The fab news is you have already become quite the expert at managing your 10 human needs. Let me provide you with a little refresher of your learning so far:

1. **Physical health** (our body's need to function): Sleep, hydrate, breathe, pee, move, rest and eat. In chapter 10 you began to experiment with new ways of looking after your body.
2. **Safety** (our need to be safe, secure and protected):

Hurrah, while your Inner Caveman may cause you some issues in your thinking, you know you can trust him, and therefore yourself, to get you to a place of safety when it really matters.

3. **Mental health** (our need to have rational beliefs, realistic thoughts and perspective): By being able to spot your Inner Caveman in action and developing your Inner Coach, you are already learning how to manage this need.

4. **Emotional health** (our need to identify and express our feelings safely): Whoop whoop, you are already recognising when you feel far from fine and learning how to express these feelings in a healthier way.

5. **Love and connection** (our need to connect with others, be loved and belong): Love and connection are beautiful things and, as social animals, we all need them.

6. **Worth** (our need to be seen and heard, to feel valued, significant and validated): In chapter 12 you will be saying goodbye to those should messages that stop you feeling worthy. You will also learn to slay your pesky self-doubt and embrace self-clout.

7. **Spiritual** (our need to follow our faith if it is part of our belief system): You know how to keep an ear out for any well-meaning but harmful should messages.

8. **Growth** (our need to learn, adapt and develop): By reading this book you are already investing in your personal growth.

9. **Cultural** (our need to follow cultural practices): Sure, follow cultural practices, but again you know to be wary of those should messages.

10. **Financial** (our need to provide resources for our other needs): We all need dosh to pay for stuff. We just don't need dosh to prove our worth.

While it may seem overwhelming to juggle so many needs, your wise Inner Coach is already well aware of what you need in most situations. For example, do you remember Great Auntie Sue? Well, imagine if you were lactose intolerant and she made you a trifle. I think your wise Inner Coach would know you need to say no because it would lead you to be physically ill. Even though you wouldn't like to see her disappointed face, you know it's what you need.

When we are truly honest with ourselves we often know what we need. That invitation to spend Christmas with our parents, the annual holiday with our extended family, the cake-baking request for the summer fete. We know the answer is no, but we often fall back into our old people-pleasing ways because we feel uncomfortable. We may feel guilty or afraid of their reaction, or we can't stand to see their disappointment. If this is the case with you, I want you to remind yourself of the following:

- Each one of us is responsible for meeting our own needs. When you neglect them, you neglect yourself. If saying yes is going to affect your safety, get you into debt, or affect your physical, emotional or mental health then saying no in that moment is far more appropriate than pleasing the other person. You aren't doing anything wrong, so drop the guilt. Your needs matter, because you matter.

- Yes, Great Auntie Sue may be disappointed you turned down her trifle, but that was not your intention. Remember, the people who truly care about us may be disappointed by our decisions but we ourselves are never a disappointment. They respect us and our decisions.

Step 2: Communicate your needs

First things first, if you do find yourself about to people-please, and you need more time to assess the situation, you are entitled to take some time to think about it. You can do this by saying something like "I will come back to you tomorrow on this because I need to think it through". Yes, being clear and direct is essential for assertive communication. The words don't have to be fancy but, whether you are saying no or setting boundaries, it's important to consider the following:

- Use clear language. This may sound obvious, but the person you are talking to is not a mind reader. Don't talk around a no or heavily hint at it.
- Being clear is kind, but saying maybe when you need to say no is unkind and unfair.
- "No" is a whole sentence.
- Show you are serious by using an appropriate tone of voice. If your tone is too soft, you may find yourself being persuaded to change your mind. If your tone is too hard, you may evoke an aggressive reaction.

- If you are face to face, show you are serious by making eye contact. If this feels too intense, look at the person's eyebrows instead.
- Provide an explanation only if you feel comfortable. Explaining to Great Auntie Sue how sick you feel after trifle will help her understand your situation. But don't feel obliged; you don't owe anyone an explanation.
- Prepare your response in advance. Do you remember in chapter 5 you identified some of your triggers for people-pleasing? Well, if you practise your response in advance it can make communicating in the moment a lot easier.

Step 3: Protect your needs

When you have identified your needs and communicated them, you may have to deal with an unhealthy backlash. This is when your Inner Coach speaks up to protect your needs. There are two common reactions that you may face:

- **The attacking and judgemental reactions**: Sometimes, people may try to scare you or invoke a guilt or shame fest to strong-arm you into meeting their needs. Some may even resort to manipulation and say they are disappointed in you or call you selfish. Defy the urge to feel shame. You are not a bad person for making this decision. You have really thought this through and have the best of intentions. Don't let your Inner Caveman beat you up; let your Inner Coach guide you through this process.

- **The won't take no for an answer reaction**: Unless the person makes concessions that will change the impact on your needs, my advice is to stick to your no. Resist the urge to be wound up, take a deep breath and give another assertive no. Don't let anyone force you into a yes. Even if Great Auntie Sue puts a big slice of trifle in front of you, just thank her for the thought but don't eat it. Why? Because if you eat it, you're teaching her to ignore your no, today and forever more.

Whatever the reaction, boundaries are key to keeping yourself emotionally safe in these conversations. Boundaries teach people how to treat us; if we let someone get away with verbally abusing us once, they will do it time and again. Start by thinking about what behaviour is and isn't acceptable to you.

For example:
- It's acceptable to be upset, angry, frustrated by my decision. It's okay to express this.
- It's not acceptable to be aggressive, passive-aggressive, deliberately hurtful or mean. If this happens, I'm going to walk away from the conversation until we can have a more constructive conversation.

Now I've shown you the three steps to managing your needs and taking assertive action, let's look at some common examples to help you really get to grips with this technique.

Example 1:

Situation: Simon is a graphic designer and receives a request from a local charity asking him to help them design their new website for free.

Awareness:
• Simon feels the urge to please and say yes, and he can already feel the guilt rising!

Brake:
• He takes himself away from his laptop and goes for a walk for 20 minutes

Coach:
• Identify: He knows he can't currently afford mentally, emotionally or financially to work for free, so he needs to say no.
• Communicate: He crafts a clear response and explains he is currently at full capacity and unable to take on work for free.
• Protect: The charity thanks him for considering the request; there is no need for him to protect his needs from an unhealthy backlash.

Example 2:

Situation: April's mother-in-law, Sandra, assumes April and her husband and three children are going to theirs for New Year's Eve again this year.

Awareness:
• April can feel herself about to let this assumption

pass by so she buys herself some time by asking her mother-in-law for a glass of water

Brake:
- April takes a few deep breaths

Coach:
- Identify: April and her husband have already been discussing this and they would like to spend this year just the five of them together.
- Communicate: When Sandra comes back, April says "Sandra, I need to talk to you about New Year's Eve. James and I have been thinking and we would like to spend it at ours with just us and the kids. As Lexi is off to university next year it feels like we want to savour this time together."
- Protect: Sandra begins to cry and tells April she can't understand why she is deliberately trying to exclude her and says she is being extremely selfish. This reaction breaks April's boundaries so she acknowledges Sandra is upset, pulls her up on the word selfish and says she thinks it's best she leaves so they can both have some space to reflect.

Example 3:
Situation: Sam's line manager asks him to stay till 10pm to work on a bid.

Awareness:
- Sam feels pressurised to say yes, especially as the rest of the team are staying

Brake:
- He recites his mantra "My needs matter"

Coach:
- Identify: Sam has promised his kids he will be home for bedtime stories as he hasn't been there all week. He knows this is important for his connection with the kids. He also knows he needs to pay the bills, but he is aware he has contributed a lot to his work and built up enough trust for this not to damage his reputation.
- Communicate: Sam replies "I'm afraid I can't work late this evening. I promised the kids I would be home tonight to read them a story. I can come in early in the morning though and make a start."
- Protect: His line manager says "No problem. Thanks for coming in early tomorrow."

Example 4:
Situation: Hannah's chatty next-door neighbour, Doreen, has arrived on her doorstep for the third time this week. When Hannah completed the awareness challenge in chapter 5, she found Doreen's chats to be one of the main triggers for her people-pleasing behaviours. Hannah has been working through the ABC technique and is now ready to try this with Doreen.

Awareness:
- Hannah knows she has fallen too many times into the people-pleasing behaviour of great listener and empathic but tends to do this too much for others

Brake:
- Hannah takes three deep breaths as Doreen continues to talk at her

Coach:
- Identify: As Hannah is working from home she finds this interaction interrupts her productivity as well as her mood, so she knows it needs to stop.
- Communicate: Hannah says "Doreen, can I just stop you there? As you know, I work from home and I'm in the middle of a project. I will pop by at the weekend for a quick chat, but I really need to get on now."
- Protect: Doreen says "Oh, of course. Let me just tell you about what Dave said to me yesterday." Hannah can sense Doreen is about to launch into 20 minutes of chat, so she again jumps in and says "As I said, Doreen, I really need to get on so I will pop by on Saturday" and starts to close the door.

As you can see from these examples, if you can engage your wise Inner Coach and take assertive action using the three steps then you will be able to focus on what you truly need.

Key aha! moments

Balancing our needs and taking assertive action is blooming difficult, which is why this chapter has been full to the brim with aha! moments. If you still have a teeny-weeny bit of doubt as to whether your needs matter then remind yourself of all you have learned here:

1. The path to assertive action is not always easy but it's always worth the effort.
2. We are all responsible for managing our own needs. When we neglect our needs, we neglect ourselves.
3. Our needs matter because we matter.
4. Looking after our needs isn't selfish; it means we are more able to look after others too.
5. In the context of human needs, assertive action is the ability to identify and communicate our needs in an appropriate, clear and respectful manner.
6. When we take assertive action, we have to be prepared for potential backlash.
7. You learned how to take assertive action by using the ABC technique:

   - **A** is for Awareness: Spot those people-pleasing behaviours
   - **B** is for Brake: Take a moment to ensure you respond, rather than react
   - **C** is for Coach: Use the three steps to respond assertively:
     - Identify your needs
     - Communicate your needs
     - Protect your needs (if you encounter backlash)

CHAPTER 12

From self-doubt to self-clout

Just be yourself.

COMMON SAYING

Just be yourself. On the face of it, those three little words trip off the tongue like water off the proverbial duck's back. Going for a job interview? Just be yourself. Want to be a great leader? Just be your authentic self. From Instagram social media influencers to personal development gurus, you hear this message time and again. Now, don't get me wrong, I'm all on board with the message, but saying it and living it are two very different things. Why is it so hard to be ourselves? Well, firstly, in order to be ourselves we have to know ourselves. On the face of it, this seems fairly simple; I mean we have been hanging out with ourselves every second since day one, so surely we are all experts on ourselves, right? Unfortunately, as you found in chapter 6, this simply isn't the case. Many of us are plagued by pesky self-doubt, which not only leads us to have a distorted view of ourselves, but also leaves us writing off our entire existence with a few irrational words, like "I'm not good enough" or "I'm worthless".

Secondly, as you learned in chapter 1, the world is obsessed with telling us who we should be, and many of us choose to disown parts of ourselves rather than deviate from that path. Therefore, knowing who we are is all very well and good, but accepting who we are, and dare I say even liking who we are, warts and all, is another thing.

Thirdly, even if we know and accept ourselves in our full imperfect glory, we still have to know how to be ourselves, in an often judgemental world, without drowning in shame; and that, my friends, is a very difficult path to tread.

Self-clout is knowing who you are, accepting who you are and being who you are in everyday life without succumbing to doing what you think you should do or getting caught up in self-doubting shame. It's a choice we all have to make, and it's a journey that takes courage.

Here's a question for you. Do you ever say to yourself "I wish I'd had the courage to be me"? If you stop for a moment and feel into that statement, what comes up for you? Grab your journal and take some time to reflect on what having self-clout would mean for you.

Getting from self-doubt to self-clout

It was early September 1987, I was 9 years old and it was my first day at a new school. My one and only memory from that day is seeing a girl walk into the classroom with blonde hair and a wide smile, and I was instantly intrigued by her. Over the next few school years, we became good friends; however, I slowly noticed there was something different going on for me than in my other friendships. I couldn't quite work out what it was, but I was becoming aware she was never far from my thoughts. As we moved into our teenage years, we entered the world of puberty and boys. I wasn't a massive fan of boys, but I thought the sensible option was just to fit in, so I kissed quite a few. The problem was, though, I just didn't like it, and it slowly started to dawn on me that I was different.

As the years passed I began to believe there was something inherently wrong with me, and carrying that feeling of shame around day in, day out was exhausting and painful. I had no one to turn to; with a 99% white middle-class intake and an emphasis on getting the school to the top of the league table, difference just wasn't a thing at school. I was also acutely aware there was no opportunity for difference at home; after all, what would the neighbours say? I was lost and very lonely so, at the age of 16, after seven long years of living with this secret, I made the decision to leave school and go to a nearby college to study where there was more diversity.

At college, I felt like I could be more me. I made friends, and I left those weird feelings behind, or so I thought. Turns out having a few drinks before the college party was a bad idea, because I kissed a girl and I liked it. I think it took both of us a little by surprise, so it wasn't until it happened again, two weeks later, that I believed it was real. My response to the second kiss? I cried, *a lot*. I'm not just talking a few tears, I'm talking those full-on sobs where you can't breathe and you feel like they will never end. Looking back, it probably wasn't the ideal response she wanted, but, after many years of pretending that part of myself didn't exist, it was overwhelming to finally admit to myself I was gay.

So, I finally had to stop denying that part of my self existed, but what then? I was soon to learn a valuable lesson. There are moments in our life where we have to make a choice to be ourselves and face the world or hide away. For me, one of those moments came when I was 17; the girl I kissed had become my girlfriend (yes, she forgave me for the sobbing) and, after a few months, we felt brave enough to tell one of our friends. We decided to tell her on the quiet stairwell at lunchtime, but as she listened her face twisted into a grimace and she quickly stood up and walked away. It gets worse. We then heard her enter the classroom next door to the stairwell and announce, to the entire room of students, our "news". I could hardly breathe as I heard the laughs and the reactions seep through the wall; it was my worst nightmare come true. The shame hit me so hard I felt winded and all I wanted to do was hide. I rose to my feet and ran down the corridor, out through the yard and found myself standing at the college gates. It was then I realised I had a choice. I could keep running away from this, I could keep denying this part of myself and drown in shame for the rest of my life or I could be me. Despite being overwhelmed with feelings, I turned around and walked back across the yard and into the classroom. The first question I received was from a boy. "Are you queer?" he said, with a wide smile, as laughter erupted from the rest of the room. "Yes," I said. The judgement, the gossip, the betrayal, the hurt stung so much that I was amazed I was still standing; but the relief of accepting myself and finally being okay with being me was priceless. And it still is, every single day.

The journey from self-doubt to self-clout is ongoing throughout our lives and takes bucketloads of courage. I think it is something we strive towards each day; some days we will be brave, and on others our fear of being judged or "found out" may get the better of us. Of course, sometimes it's not safe to be ourselves, but we have to be able to know the difference between a genuine threat and our Inner Caveman kicking off. It's not an easy path to tread but there is no doubt the more we strive to be ourselves in the small and big moments in life, the happier and healthier we will be.

 Nothing makes my heart soar more than listening to stories of people making the journey from self-doubt to self-clout. When they dare to be themselves with their nearest and dearest or take the plunge to be their true self online, it is truly inspiring.

I'm sure you have already done this at times in your life, so I want you to take a moment to

reflect on some of the stories that make up the adventure that is your life journey to date. I bet they are quite incredible. I wonder if they make you feel as emotional as I feel when I think of my stories?

Your journey to self-clout

Congratulations! You are already well on your way to making the journey to self-clout. In chapter 6 you got to grips with your self-doubt and learned how to spot your limiting beliefs. In chapter 8 you embraced your Inner Coach and laid the groundwork for challenging those beliefs. Then in chapter 9 you learned how to safely express self-doubting shame from within.

All this work is invaluable in equipping you to slay self-doubt. However, there are a few more things you need to learn to set yourself up for success.

Yep, I've gone and said the S word. When I say success, I don't mean success as in earn loads of money and own a house and a car. Instead, I prefer to use this definition by Tom Bilyeu:

Success is how you feel about yourself, when you are by yourself.

For me, this definition encapsulates the aim of self-clout. When you can sit by yourself and be free of those limiting beliefs and accept yourself, warts and all, that is when you reap the benefits of all your hard work. It shows you have stopped listening to all those shoulds and you are living life on your terms.

To help you attain this success, you are going to work through several exercises created to help you know, accept and be yourself in the world. However, before you start this work, let's check your expectations. These exercises may require you to go deeper than you have gone before. When you search deep within you can find your inner treasure, but you may also stumble across a few unwanted items. Therefore, as you explore deeper, it will be natural to feel uncomfortable at times.

To help you through these exercises I want you to draw on your learnings from previous chapters. Specifically, I want you to remember the ABC technique: Awareness, Brake, Coach.

Be **A**ware of your:
- Inner Caveman kicking off
- Feelings filling up your emotional bucket
- Body sensations going into overdrive

If you notice any of these then I want you to apply an emergency **B**rake. This can be as simple as taking three long, deep breaths or going for a walk. However, if this isn't enough, please set the exercises aside and take some time out to properly care for yourself.

Then, when you feel more settled, engage your Inner Coach. If the exercise brings up uncomfortable feelings, can you draw on the learnings from chapter 9 to help? Is there anyone you trust who you can talk to about the exercise or can you take 15 minutes to write about it? If your body feels tense or anxious, can you use your practices to shift yourself into a calmer state? Would 10 minutes of stretching or meditation help?

Lastly, if your Inner Caveman starts kicking off with any of those unhelpful thoughts, I want you to remind yourself of your previous work. For example, this negative voice may try to discount some of your positive attributes or may start comparing you with others in the "Yeah, but Geoff has loads more qualifications than I do" type of way. If it does so, remember these are unhelpful and negative thought types:

- Discounting the positive
- Comparison

Use your Inner Coach to take a step back and gain a more rational perspective. Remember, there is no right or wrong in these exercises; we are all different.

Often the most profound change comes when we step into our courage, so when you are ready, take a deep breath, and let's begin.

How to know yourself

First up you are going to look beyond those limiting beliefs and connect to your true self by completing the **I** exercise again. The aims of this exercise are to:

- Demonstrate the complexity of humans and prove to your Inner Caveman that you can't be summed up by a phrase (limiting belief) such as "I'm not good enough". Instead, equip your wise Inner Coach with ample evidence to commit to new realistic beliefs.
- Reconnect to your true self to help your Inner Coach fight off judgement from others.

In chapter 1 I invited you to draw a capital **I** and write in it all the should messages that have been thrown at you in life. This time I'm going to ask you to draw a capital **I** and fill it to the brim with all aspects of your true self, warts and all. Self-clout isn't about pretending you are the most amazing person in the world; neither is it buying into a story that you are the worst person in the world. This is an exercise to help you see past those irrational limiting beliefs and connect with your true self.

Most people don't have a problem writing down their warts, but become stuck writing down their positive attributes, skills and contributions, so I've included some prompts to help you. Please take your time with this exercise as there is no rush.

The **I** exercise

First off, grab yourself a piece of paper and some coloured pens and draw a capital **I**. To get some inspiration before you start this exercise, check out my own **I**.

Now read through the prompts below and start to fill your **I** with all those things that make you so very you. Feel free to be as creative as you like, and don't forget to pause between each prompt to reflect or take a break.

Exercise prompts

1. Write your name and then, if you feel comfortable, add your gender, race, ethnicity, age, nationality, sexuality and any distinguishing roles you want to add, such as mum, daughter, friend.

2. State your eye colour, hair colour, height; those physical attributes that make you you.

3. Identify your two or three key values:
   - Your values are the beliefs that define what is most important to you.
   - For example: contribution, loyalty, family, growth, service, justice, love, adventure.

4. Describe your traits and qualities:
   - For example: kind, funny, responsible, thoughtful, flexible, frugal, sensitive, honest, loyal, generous, ambitious, determined, gentle.
   - If you find this difficult, ask a trusted friend or colleague to identify the qualities they value in you. Sometimes we are so used to discounting our qualities that we become blind to them, so asking others is a fab way to reconnect to ourselves.

5. Add your skills:
    - For example: empathic, listening, decisive, communication, organisational, management, craft making, caring, mediation, meditation, baking.

6. List your interests:
    - For example: sports, hiking, gaming, TV and film, meditation, family time, adventure, travel.

7. Include your qualifications:
    - For example: school, college, university or specific professional certificates.

8. Analyse the contribution you have made in relationships, jobs and life in general:
    - For example: at work, you may have helped build a team, contributed to a project, sold work, supported a colleague.
    - With friends, you may have been a shoulder to cry on, helped X with their job application.
    - At home, you may contribute to the running of the house with time and/or money, offer support to others.

9. Reflect on your life experiences; what have you learned?
    - For example: how to set boundaries, how to overcome adversity, how to look after yourself.

10. Lastly, add those warts. The aspects of your true self you would prefer to hide. We are all fallible human beings and none of us are perfect, so let's be honest about those warts:
    - For example: snappy when tired, lose temper when stressed, comfort eat when sad.

Once you have spent some time on this, set it aside for a few days and come back to it with fresh eyes. All masterpieces take time to create, so give yourself the time and space you need for this exercise.

. . . .

The I exercise: Check-in

Before you move on, I want to check in with you. How are you feeling? As I said earlier, it's not uncommon for the I exercise to bring up a variety of thoughts and feelings, so if this is the case then put the book down and take some time out. Nourish your brain and body, give it what it needs to reset and then – and only then – continue to the next section.

The I exercise: Reflection

I was going to write that now you have *completed* the I exercise, take some time to reflect on what you have learned from it, but of course this exercise is never really finished. As we are ever-growing beings, each day we grow in some way: a new experience, new information, a new skill. Not only does this mean this exercise is never really complete, but it also means no piece of paper is ever going to be large enough to truly reflect you. As I write this, I'm 42 years old, which is over fifteen thousand days where I have grown in some way. That's a whole lot of stuff to fit onto an A4-sized piece of paper.

Bear this in mind when you think about the aims of the exercise and take some time to reflect:

Aim 1: *Demonstrate the complexity of humans and prove to your Inner Caveman that you can't be summed up by a phrase (limiting belief) such as "I'm not good enough". Instead equip your wise Inner Coach with ample evidence to commit to new realistic beliefs.*

As you made your way through the prompts and began to explore the various aspects of your true self, were you able to see how complex us humans really are? Did it prove to you that no one can be summed up by a phrase like "I'm not good enough" or "I'm a bad person"?

Even if the exercise felt uncomfortable or you found it difficult to fill your drawing, did it reveal some surprises? Did it reconnect you to parts of yourself you had forgotten about? Can you see how your vast array of skills, qualities and experiences, and even your warts, make you, beautifully and uniquely, you? If so, does this new perspective mean your Inner Coach is ready to create some new beliefs?

Aim 2: *Reconnect to your true self to help your Inner Coach fight off judgement from others.*

You will learn how to ward off judgement in the final section, but for now do you notice how being connected to your true self helps you feel more grounded? I often use the analogy of a tree and its roots. When a tree has strong roots, no matter the strength of wind it will remain upright. Yes, it may sway but it doesn't get knocked down by the wind. I think people are like this too. When we have a strong sense of our true self, warts and all, it provides a grounding that can support us in the face of a whirlwind of judgement.

 Take some time to reflect here on how it feels to be more connected to you.

Phew! It's a lot to digest, isn't it? However, if you spend time really thinking this through then you are far less likely to fall back into your self-doubting ways. Getting to know yourself, warts and all, can be scary, but I hope you have found there is so much more to you than your Inner Caveman ever let you think. Connecting with your true self is truly a game-changer for your health and happiness levels.

How to accept yourself

Now you have had time to reflect on the **I** exercise, hopefully you will have found those old limiting beliefs no longer serve you. This means it's time to commit to some new beliefs. As you learned in chapter 8, new thoughts take time to form, and this is true for new beliefs too. However, by committing to these beliefs today you are sowing the seeds for tomorrow.

Exercise 1: New belief

Let's start by replacing that old not good enough or similar belief or phrase. Grab yourself a pen and paper and write out your old belief. When you are done, I want you to scribble it out. Completely. Now it's time for your wise Inner Coach to write down your new belief.

For example:
- Old belief: "I'm not good enough"
- New belief: "I'm an ever-growing imperfectly perfect human being"

Can you accept this new belief about yourself? Remember, this isn't pretending you are the best person in the world, and it certainly doesn't let you lower your standards. If this new belief doesn't quite fit then take some time here to find the right words for you.

Exercise 2: A life without shoulds

Next, I want you to think about the "Are you shoulding all over yourself?" exercise you completed in chapter 1. Here you also drew an **I** and filled it with all the should messages you've internalised. When you compare these two drawings can you see how different they are? Can you commit to letting go of those should messages and accept who you are now? Will you take responsibility for your growth going forward?

To help you with this, think about repeating the **I** exercise from this chapter in three years' time:
* What additional skills, interests or qualities do you want to be writing in your **I**?
* Do you want to be writing less about who others think you should be?
* Do you want to be listing less of the things others think you should do?

I believe we can only truly accept ourselves, and therefore be ourselves, in this world when we commit to letting go of listening to those shoulds and stop chasing our worth. So, can you make a commitment today to coach yourself to do what you want to do and be who you want to be? By making this commitment you are empowering your Inner Coach to guide you to a life you want, putting you in control and enhancing your mental, emotional and physical health.

To enable you to keep to these new beliefs and commitments, I want you to write them down somewhere you can see them, such as in a prominent place in your journal or on a sticky note on your mirror as a reminder. Here are a few examples:
* I'm an ever-growing imperfectly perfect human being
* I'm no longer listening to the shoulds
* I'm going to be me and do what is healthy for me
* I'm good enough
* My worth isn't dependent on what others think
* I'm going to follow my own path

Whatever words you decide on, writing them down and saying them loud and proud will help you on your journey to self-acceptance.

How to be yourself

Of course, knowing and accepting yourself is one thing but being yourself, in an often judgemental world, is quite another. After many years of working in this field, I have found the key to being yourself in this world is mastering the art of self-validation. I define this as the practice of checking in truthfully with ourselves when faced with judgement, whether it comes from others or ourselves. Let's explore this further using the ABC technique.

A is for Awareness

As I'm sure you are aware, when we are ourselves in the world, we are more vulnerable to receiving unpleasant feedback, judgement and nasty comments. This can come from loved ones, friends, acquaintances, total strangers and even ourselves. When we receive this commentary, we instantly begin to absorb the words and this triggers a shame response, which in turn hampers our ability to respond rationally. Therefore, before we can start to validate ourselves, we need to defuse this shame. As soon as you become aware of this powerful feeling, I want you to move on to step B.

B is for Brake

Shame causes a similar physiological reaction in our body to anxiety, which means it will flood us with feelings and hormones that make us want to shut down (or in my case hide under the duvet). If you become aware of a feeling of shame, apply your emergency brake by taking a moment to breathe, walk or ground yourself. Taking a little time out here to calm your brain and body will mean you are less likely to react by:

- Holding yourself back from opportunities
- Being inauthentic by trying too hard to fit in
- Perfecting and procrastinating
- Seeking external validation

C is for Coach: Practising self-validation

Responding to judgement from others

When you feel settled, I want you to visualise the person who provided this judgement. Imagine they are throwing a ball at you. This ball contains their words. You know that if you don't respond the ball is going to hit you and it's going to hurt. So, I want you to catch the ball in your mind's eye and then examine the words and ask yourself:

- Does this person have my best interests at heart?
- Am I doing anything wrong?
- Am I wrong?

The first question leads you to explore why this person is giving you this information. It allows you to filter out judgement from people who are only saying things in order to hurt you, thus providing a protective barrier around you.

The next question encourages your Inner Coach to take a step back and explore the situation. We all have the ability to step outside of our integrity at times or make a mistake. When you *do* do something wrong you need to take responsibility for your actions and make amends. This question also invites your Inner Coach to learn from the situation rather than letting your Inner Caveman beat you up.

Spoiler alert: The answer to "Am I wrong?" is always no. However, ask it to safeguard yourself from getting caught up in old limiting beliefs and shame. Use it to connect you to your true self and remind you of your new beliefs and commitments.

Let's look at four examples to understand how this works.

Example 1:
Situation: Davinder received a tweet from Lionface406 on Twitter. Yesterday, Davinder tweeted about his recent job promotion. This morning he received a reply from Lionface406: "Stop showing off about your job promotion, some of us haven't even got a job."

Awareness:

- Davinder immediately feels a pang of shame. He wants to react and delete his tweet, but he recognises the shame and decides to apply his emergency brake.

Brake:

- To stop himself reacting, he takes himself away for a 30-minute walk

Coach:

On returning he engages his Inner Coach and imagines Lionface406 throwing his phone at him. He catches the phone, examines the tweet and asks himself:

- Does Lionface406 really have my best interests at heart? No, I don't even know Lionface406. They just wanted someone to vent their anger at and today it was my unlucky day.
- Have I done anything wrong? It's okay to celebrate my success and publically thank those who helped me. I haven't done anything to feel guilty about.
- Am I wrong? No. I have no reason to feel shame. My worth is not dependent on what others think I should and shouldn't do.

This example shows how we can ward off judgement by giving our Inner Coach time to respond. By taking time out, Davinder was quickly able to see this person didn't have his best interests at heart. Even though he would have preferred not to have received the comment, he was able to recover quickly and respond in a healthy way.

Example 2:
Situation: Jade's housemate Lydia told her she was selfish and a terrible friend for not taking the day off work to celebrate her birthday.

Awareness:
- The word selfish hit Jade like a slap in the face. Her Mum used to call her this growing up and she can feel the sting of shame rise up in her body.

Brake:
- She takes some long, deep breaths

Coach:
She engages her Inner Coach, catches the words and asks herself:
- Does Lydia have my best interests at heart? Usually she is really kind, but I know her boyfriend has just split up with her and she is hitting out because she is sad.
- Have I done anything wrong? She didn't ask me to take the day off and I really needed to work today as my monthly report is due. She was in the wrong for calling me selfish. I'm going to talk to her about it tomorrow.
- Am I wrong? I can hear my Inner Caveman wanting to label me as selfish and twist the words terrible friend into my old belief that I'm a bad person. However, I know that it's not true. I know I have contributed to our friendship over the years and I'm not a terrible person. I am not perfect by any means, but I'm doing

my best and I'm proud of who I am now and who I'm becoming.

Poor Jade found her best friend's comments painful but, rather than reacting from a hurt place, she was able to breathe and give her Inner Coach time to respond in a healthy way. She didn't entertain her old limiting belief and she reminded herself of her new beliefs.

Responding to judgement from ourselves

If we notice our Inner Caveman causing shame to rise in us, we need our Inner Coach to filter our own words.

Example 3:
Situation: Kate made a mistake at work and sent out an email to her client instead of her boss, and her Inner Caveman screamed "I'm not good enough!"

Awareness:
- Kate notices her Inner Caveman has made a fleeting return and she feels the shame rising within

Brake:
- She uses the 5-4-3-2-1 grounding practice to calm her body

Coach:
She engages her Inner Coach, catches the words and asks herself:
- Does my Inner Caveman have my best interests

at heart? Jester, my Inner Caveman, wants me to survive but this is not a life-threatening situation and his reaction is therefore really unhelpful!

- Have I done anything wrong? Yes, I've made a mistake, which is going to cause a few issues. I feel upset, and guilty; however, I know I can trust myself to rectify the situation.
- Am I wrong? No. I am a fallible human being, I'm imperfectly perfect and I'm doing my best. It doesn't mean I'm not good enough. That one mistake doesn't wipe out all those values, skills, experiences, qualifications and contributions. It doesn't mean I'm a bad person or bad at my job.

As you can see, Kate was able to notice that old limiting belief creeping back and dismiss it by grounding herself in her skills, values, traits and other positive qualities.

Example 4:
Situation: It's 9:15pm and Cat is still putting the finishing touches to her assignment. She's been doing this for three hours. She can hear her Inner Critic screaming "It should be perfect!"

Awareness:
- Cat knows she is trying to perfect and can feel shame rising, so she realises she needs to take a moment

Brake:
- She mindfully makes a cup of tea and takes a moment to close her eyes

Coach:

She engages her Inner Coach, catches the words and asks herself:

- Does my Inner Cavewoman really have my best interests at heart? I know Perfect Pearl, my Inner Critic, wants to achieve high standards, but her relentless screaming is pushing me to exhaustion and I need to stop.
- Have I done anything wrong? No. The piece isn't perfect but it's more than good enough to submit. It has everything I wanted to write; it's not quite as short as I wanted but it's within the word count and good enough to be submitted now.
- Am I wrong? No. I'm imperfectly perfect and I'm good enough. I'm more than one essay and I know I am loved for more than my grades.

Cat is able to notice her perfecting behaviour and question her Inner Critic. She is able to break free from this behaviour by letting her Inner Coach ask these three simple questions.

As you can see from these examples, self-validation is our compassionate Inner Coach taking a step back and analysing the judgement. It doesn't let us off the hook when we get something wrong, but it doesn't ever let us believe we are wrong. By catching judgement, and asking these questions, we can filter the content and create a shield around us so we can safely be ourselves in the world.

While the above technique is simple, it is far from easy to master. Each situation requires you to remember to catch the judgement, calm yourself and work through it. At first you'll wrestle with this process, and those questions, but over time you'll notice how your Inner Coach becomes quicker at responding. Then one day you'll notice a judgemental comment from your neighbour and you'll automatically respond in a healthy manner. There is no greater feeling than being able to be yourself in the world, and if you commit the effort to following the practice of self-validation, this way of being is available to you.

Key aha! moments

Now, I know what you are thinking ... Well okay, I don't because I can't mind read, but I reckon your brain is a little crammed full of stuff, so feel free to go make a strong decaf tea or whatever floats your boat. When you are fully back in the learning zone, reacquaint yourself with this beautiful and bold chapter on self-clout:

1. Self-clout is knowing who we are, accepting who we are and being who we are in everyday life without succumbing to doing what we think we should do or drowning in shame.
2. The road to self-clout is difficult, but it releases us from shame and can feel awesome.
3. Knowing our values, traits, skills, qualifications, life experiences, contributions, nationality, sexuality,

gender, relationships, and more can help us to connect to who we really are.

4. Humans are very complex and cannot be summed up in a simple phrase such as bad person, I'm not good enough, failure.

5. Making a commitment to new beliefs and living a life without shoulds is the path to self-acceptance.

6. The key to being ourselves in the world is being able to validate ourselves.

7. Self-validation is the practice of checking in truthfully with ourselves when faced with judgement, whether that judgement comes from others or ourselves. To do this we use the ABC technique:

- **A** is for Awareness: Notice when shame rears its ugly head
- **B** is for Brake: Calm your brain and body to let the shame subside
- **C** is for Coach: Respond by self-validating. Visualise the person who provided this judgement. Imagine they are throwing a ball at you. This ball contains their words. You know that if you don't respond the ball is going to hit you and it's going to hurt. So, catch the ball in your mind's eye and then examine the words and ask yourself:
  - ◦ Does this person have my best interests at heart?
  - ◦ Am I doing anything wrong?
  - ◦ Am I wrong? (The answer to this is always no!)

CHAPTER 13

Healthy ever after

The biggest factor that determines our health and happiness
is how we talk to ourselves, and coach ourselves,
through our daily life.

ZOE CLEMENTS

As a kid, I used to love watching movies with epic happy
ever afters. At the time, I didn't have a clue why I felt
anxious or had an annoying negative voice in my head;
all I knew was that those films filled me with the hope
that one day I would be free of all my crappiness and
ride off into a beautiful sunset. It felt such a relief. Never
once did it occur to me to think about what happened to
those characters after the credits rolled. I mean, surely
even the cast of *Dirty Dancing* would have no choice
but to cancel their end-of-season show in the midst of
a pandemic?

So, as much as Brian thinks I *should* end this book with
a happy ever after, my Inner Coach is wise enough to
know it's just not that simple. What I can offer you, though,
is the very thing I really needed from those happy ever
after movies: hope.

As you know, this book was never about fixing you so that you could ride off into the sunset. Life is not a Hollywood movie; it's more a complex journey full of twists and turns. Some days will be full of joy and excitement; a birth, a wedding or those beautiful ordinary moments with loved ones. Other days, you may be being made redundant, or need to face a gigantic life-changing event you never saw coming. However, what this book does give you is the power to respond to whatever life throws at you next. You can choose how you talk to yourself and you can use the techniques and practices to help yourself. So, while I can't end this book on a happy ever after, I can set you on a course towards *healthy ever after*. Before we say our final goodbye, I have a few more aha! moments to offer you, to help you on your journey of growth beyond this last chapter.

The final aha! moments

Final aha! 1: Always make time to reflect on how far you have come

"We have a long way to go," sighed the boy.
"Yes, but look how far we have come," said the horse.

CHARLIE MACKESY

I have this quote, and accompanying illustration, on the wall of my counselling room. It serves as a reminder to my clients of how far they have come. This moment of reflection is not only food for the soul, it's an invitation to your Inner Coach to own its actions. I invite you to start this practice now, by congratulating yourself on reading this book. Give yourself a blooming great big pat on the back. You took up the challenge, stepped into your courage, made it through the rollercoaster of awareness and signed on the dotted line to commit to change. That, my friend, is cause for celebration, so recognise your efforts, acknowledge your courage and perseverance, own them and reward yourself. Seriously, treat yourself to a massage, give yourself a glass of bubbles or take an hour to just relax in the bath. Whatever you do, mark this achievement and be proud, because you have invested in yourself and you, my friend, are truly awesome.

 Note: If there wasn't a pause of at least five minutes between reading the last paragraph and this one then you moved on way too quickly, so I will say it again: take some time to reflect on this journey, grab your journal and look back at all you have learned and achieved.

Final aha! 2: Failure is the best kind of feedback

Do the best you can until you know better. Then when you know better, do better.

MAYA ANGELOU

In this book I have touched upon two truths about humans:

- We are ever-growing beings and have the ability, and the choice, to adapt, learn and develop
- Human beings are fallible

While these facts aren't going to come up as a question in a pub quiz any time soon, they are helpful to understand because, when put together, they point to another inevitable truth that will help you: you are going to fail and fall back into old ways. However, if you can learn from these mistakes then change will be quicker and more sustainable. So, when you find yourself slipping back into old patterns of thinking, feeling or behaving, don't let your Inner Caveman judge you; instead, engage your Inner Coach and learn from the setback. Remind yourself that tomorrow is another day, and tomorrow you can take that learning and try again.

Make the commitment to this practice now. Trust me, if you can view all failure as merely feedback then you will save yourself a whole lot of anguish.

Final aha! 3: Always maintain your practice

There is no glory in practice but without practice there is no glory.

ZOE'S YOGA TEACHER

My yoga teacher used to throw out nuggets of life wisdom while we were mid pose. As we were in a not-so-comfortable 40-degree heated room, I missed much of the wisdom, but one that did resonate was about needing to maintain our practice. She stated that the hardest phase of doing anything is maintenance. She was right; I gave up my wobbly hot yoga after six long months because I didn't have the dedication to maintain my practice.

While you have gained lots of self-awareness and learned many new techniques, you need to remain committed to continuing to change. The most effective method for keeping your learning alive is to regularly check in with yourself. While I couldn't maintain my hot yoga practice, my relationship of 14 years with my now wife continues to thrive because we found a way to navigate the maintenance phase. We do this by regularly checking in with each other and adjusting life accordingly. Sometimes these conversations are fun, sometimes they are hard, but they are always more than worth it because they refocus us on our goal and put us back on the right path to achieving it. Therefore, to help you continue towards your goal of living a happier and healthier life, I encourage you to embrace the following check-in practice.

The reflection check-in

Check-ins in life aren't just reserved for birthdays or New Year's Eve; they need to be done regularly to keep us on track. Therefore, for the next 12 weeks at least,

I want you to set an alarm in your phone or mark your calendar to remind you to check in with yourself once a week. Don't worry, this doesn't require you to book into a silent retreat for the weekend or stare out to sea for three hours. Just set aside 30 minutes for some quiet, uninterrupted reflection time to check in with yourself. When you are there, I want you to use your trusty ABC technique to help you:

A is for Awareness
Bring some awareness to your journey:

What's been working well?
- How loud is your Inner Coach?
- Are you safely expressing your feelings?
- Is your body feeling calmer for longer?
- Are you saying no and taking assertive action?
- Are you being yourself and practising self-validation?

What's not been working so well?
- Is your Inner Caveman noisy?
- Are you feeling overwhelmed or stuck?
- How anxious have you been?
- Any people-pleasing behaviours?
- Have you noticed yourself slipping into self-doubt?

B is for Brake
As always, take a moment to ground yourself and let the thoughts and feelings raised by these questions gently subside.

C is for Coach

Ask yourself what adjustments you need to make to put yourself back on track. Do you need to:

- Revisit any of the awareness exercises or ABC techniques?
- Work on your Inner Coach's voice and practise rational thinking and finding a fresh perspective?
- Express your feelings more?
- Reach out for your Anxiety First Aid Kit or plan in some more calm time?
- Identify your needs better and express them more?
- Practise self-validation or revisit your **I** exercise?

Reflecting on your progress not only keeps you on track, but it also creates a habit of checking in with yourself. This habit will signal to your brain that this is important, and by the end of the 12 weeks, you will start to do this check-in naturally.

As I stated in the introduction, this book is now your pocket guide for life. You can find a reminder of all the ABC techniques in the Appendix, but don't be afraid to delve back into other chapters, as and when you need to.

The final aha! The most important aha! of all

As you have read the book from cover to cover I think you have earned the right to hear the most important aha! of all. While helping people become healthier versions of themselves and seeing this ripple out into the world is the most rewarding part of counselling for me, it isn't the reason why I love counselling. You see, when you truly sit with someone in their suffering, when you really listen to them and empathise with them, something remarkable occurs. Defence mechanisms start to lower, trust builds up and slowly their heart and soul shine through with all the breathtaking beauty of an epic sunrise.

Over the years, I have noticed, as each heart and soul emerge, how unique they are and how they leave their own elegant print on mine, and the world. I'm grateful for this every day because, when things get tough in my own life, it reminds me how we all have a unique print we leave on those around us, whether we realise it or not. It reminds me I'm worthy, not for what I do but for my very being.

So, the final aha! is this: you are not your job, your pay packet or your body image. You are your heart and soul, *you are worthy* and you matter. Every. Single. Day.

Always remember you matter, you're important and you are loved, and you bring to this world things no one else can.

CHARLIE MACKESY

Final words

Every evening as I retire to the sofa, Paddy jumps on my lap for a cuddle and then promptly falls asleep like he doesn't have a care in the world. Although chasing squirrels and rolling in mud is indeed tiring work, he just doesn't have the stresses and strains that come with being human. While I still sometimes envy his simple little life, these days I feel much happier in my own. Not only did my time in the counselling room, as both client and counsellor, help me to understand that panic attack I had aged 10, it also provided the awareness and practices I need to deal with what life throws my way. My wish was to create a book that would pass this learning on to others, so I hope you find yourself sleeping a little easier at night too.

It's been an absolute honour and a privilege to serve you, so thank you for trusting me to be your guide on this journey. I've loved writing every word. Over at **zoeclements.co.uk** you can find more of my work, including free resources, blogs and information on counselling with me. You can also sign up to hear more from Paddy and me. We'd love to keep in touch.

Till next time.

All the best,

Zoe

Appendix

Between stimulus and response there is a space.
In that space is our power to choose our response.
In our response lies our growth and our freedom.

VIKTOR FRANKL

The ABC techniques

Your power lies in how you respond to a situation. To help you on your ongoing journey to living a healthier and happier life, on the next pages is a quick reminder of all the ABC techniques in the book that will help you do just that.

How to think like a coach

A is for Awareness: Recognise unhelpful thought types:

- Labelling: I'm an idiot
- Mind reading: They think I'm stupid
- Catastrophising: I've missed the train, so I'm going to lose my job
- Shoulds: I should be perfect
- Phoneyism: I'm an imposter
- Overgeneralising: Everything is terrible
- Comparison: They have a much better life than me
- Discounting the positive: I only got the job as no one else applied
- "What if ...?" thoughts: What if this happens? What if that happens?

B is for Brake: Calm your brain so you can access your rational thinking brain (aka your Inner Coach)

C is for Coach: Challenge unhelpful thoughts and develop a rational perspective using four practices:

- Judge and jury: Use evidence to provide rational thought
- Helicopter view: Zoom out and look at the bigger picture
- What would Thomas Edison do? Learn from failure and try again
- The Goldilocks approach to worrying: Just the right amount

How to feel fab

A is for Awareness: Recognise when you are gripped by a feeling or overwhelmed

B is for Brake: Calm your brain and body so you don't react in old ways

C is for Coach: Respond by choosing the most appropriate way to safely express those hard-to-shift feelings:

- Use motion to shift emotion: A walk in nature, yoga, stretching, running, weight lifting
- Expressing feelings through writing: Expressive writing for 15 minutes or journaling
- Embracing The Beatles: Get a little help from your friends: Empty your emotional bucket by calling on a person you trust and expressing yourself
- Embracing The Beatles: Help, I need somebody: Call a helpline or find a counsellor for those more stubborn feelings

How to relieve anxiety in the moment

A is for Awareness: Notice the physical signs of anxiety:

- Uncomfortable, fast heartbeat
- Short, quick breaths into your chest
- Stomach churning or fluttering, often called butterflies, leading you to need the loo more
- Tensed muscles
- Difficulty concentrating and poor memory
- Sweaty, with heat creeping up your body
- Nauseous
- Wobbly legs
- Dry mouth, difficulty in swallowing
- Wide, dilated eyes

B is for Brake: Calm your brain and body

C is for Coach: Respond by using the Anxiety First Aid Kit:

- Belly breathing
- 5-4-3-2-1 grounding technique
- Taking a walk
- Looking at pictures of loved ones
- Solving puzzles
- Mindfulness
- Stretching

and check in with your thoughts and feelings!

How to manage your needs and take assertive action

A is for Awareness: Spot your people-pleasing behaviours:

- Saying yes when you need to say no
- Avoiding conflict like the plague
- Avoiding giving feedback or an opinion
- Difficulty in setting boundaries or maintaining boundaries
- Difficulty in making decisions involving others
- Being a great listener and empathic but tending to do this too much for others
- Finding being assertive difficult
- Putting tasks for others before self-caring

B is for Brake: Calm your brain and body so you don't react in old ways

C is for Coach: Respond by:

1. Identifying your needs
2. Communicating your needs by being clear and kind
3. Protecting your needs (if you encounter backlash)

How to be yourself, in a judgemental world, without drowning in shame

A is for Awareness: Notice shame rising in your emotional bucket and body

B is for Brake: Calm your brain and body till the shame subsides

C is for Coach: Respond by self-validating:

- Visualise the person who provided this judgement
- Imagine they are throwing a ball at you. This ball contains their words. You know that if you don't respond the ball is going to hit you and it's going to hurt. So, catch the ball in your mind's eye and then examine the words and ask yourself:
  - Does this person have my best interests at heart?
  - Am I doing anything wrong?
  - Am I wrong? (The answer to this is always no!)

How to maintain your practice and journey to living a healthier and happier life

A is for Awareness: Check in with yourself each week and bring awareness to:

* What's been working well?
* What's not been working so well?

B is for Brake: If these questions bring up uncomfortable thoughts or feelings then calm your brain and body

C is for Coach: Respond by asking yourself what adjustments you need to make to put yourself back on track. Do you need to:

* Revisit any of the awareness exercises or ABC techniques?
* Work on your Inner Coach's voice and practise rational thinking and finding a fresh perspective?
* Express your feelings more?
* Reach out for your Anxiety First Aid Kit or plan in some more calm time?
* Identify your needs better and express them more?
* Practise self-validation or revisit your **I** exercise?

Zoe Clements, MBACP (Accred), PGDip, is a qualified integrative counsellor and an accredited member of the British Association for Counselling and Psychotherapy. Since beginning her training in 2003 she has worked in various settings including helplines, schools and charities and from her own private practice in London.

Zoe specialises in helping others soothe their brain and ease their anxiety and offers counselling to clients in person as well as online. As a recovered overthinker, she is passionate about raising awareness of anxiety through professional speaking events, blogging and social media. When she is not working she can be found travelling or in South East London, where she lives with her wife, Lucinda, and their dog, Paddy.

Find out more about Zoe and her counselling services at **zoeclements.co.uk/counselling**

Printed in Great Britain
by Amazon